HOW TO READ SHOP DRAWINGS

with
Special Reference
to
Welding and Welding Symbols

Welding Symbols as Standardized by The American
Welding Society

THE LINCOLN ELECTRIC COMPANY
CLEVELAND, OHIO 44117

LINCOLN ELECTRIC COMPANY OF CANADA, LTD.
Leaside, Toronto 17, Ontario, Canada

LINCOLN ELECTRIC COMPANY (AUSTRALIA) PTY., LTD.
P.O. Box 22, Padstow, New South Wales

LINCOLN ELECTRIC COMPANY (EUROPE) S.A.
Grand Quevilly, (SM), France

EXPORT REPRESENTATIVES
International Division Armco Steel Corporation
Middletown, Ohio, U.S.A.

CONTENTS

HOW TO READ SHOP DRAWINGS

SHOP DRAWINGS — or BLUEPRINTS — or ENGINEERING DRAWINGS — are *not* just mysterious collections of lines and symbols and numbers on pieces of white or blue or brown paper designed to confuse people in shops. Neither are they a foreign language that can be learned only through long years of sweat and struggle.

They *are* a language, however, and one that is fairly easy to learn. They are a system of word-pictures which the designer of an object, or of a piece of equipment, uses to communicate his ideas to the man or woman who is going to build the object, or assemble the equipment, or to maintain and repair it.

The designer uses a *shop drawing* to show these other people exactly what shapes and sizes the parts of the object are to have, and what relationships each part has to the other parts — how they are to fit together. By reading the drawings, the worker in the shop can learn quickly just what the designer wants him to do — what shape each part is to have, what all of its dimensions are to be, how it fits together with the other parts — and *how it is to be welded together with these other parts.*

As a weldor, you will be welding parts together. You will be fabricating many kinds of objects of metal. You may be helping to manufacture tools or machinery, or industrial production equipment of many kinds. You may be building bridges or ships, factories or homes, automobiles or space-ships. You may be repairing, maintaining or remodeling machines and equipment of many kinds. You will be an important person in almost any industry you go into.

Wherever you are, you will be truly valuable to your employer *only* if you can read this language of shop drawings and can know what these drawings are telling you to do with the parts and materials on the shop floor or work bench in front of you.

As a weldor who has learned to read prints and drawings quickly and accurately, you can be the person who not only gets the interesting and challenging jobs to do, but also the *best-paying* jobs in the shop. You also can be the first person considered for *promotion* when supervisors are needed — because you have shown that you not only know *how* to do the welding itself, but you also know *where* and *why* the designer, and your employer, want it done.

This book is designed to help you learn to read the language of the shop drawing. It will *not* teach you how to make the drawing. You have learned how to read this book without knowing how to set the type, or to run the printing press. And you can learn, just as easily, how to read a shop drawing without

1

being able to make the drawing. You will not learn from this book how to make each type of figure or line — except where such knowledge will help you to read the drawing and to understand what the designer is trying to say to you. You *will* learn what the various kinds of lines and figures *mean*, and you will be able to follow the instructions they are giving you.

PICTURE DRAWINGS

Instead of starting with actual lines and angles, etc., let's look first at a simple drawing itself. We will try to see *what* it is saying to us, and then we will work back to the details of *how* it is telling us these things. Let's look at a simple welded base, made of several lengths of angle iron, shown in *Figure 1*. We find that there are two general ways by which we can illustrate this base — with a picture drawing, or with a mechanical or engineering drawing.

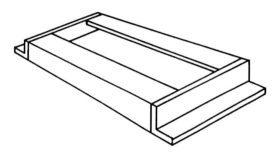

Fig. 1 — Perspective drawing of a simple welded base

Picture drawings themselves can be divided into two general classes: true pictures called *perspective* drawings, or somewhat distorted pictures called *isometric* or oblique or cabinet drawings. Picture drawings are very useful in showing us what the object will look like as we see it in front of us when it is completed. But they do not help us much in actually fabricating the object because they are not drawn to *scale* and do not give us accurate

dimensions, nor accurate locations of important details.

The familiar picture of a railroad track running away into the distance illustrates the *perspective* drawing. The rails seem to get closer together; and the ties appear to get shorter and shorter as we look further down the track, even though we know that they are all the same length. Now note the way the sides of the welded base in *Figure 1* seem to move closer together, and the side rails seem to get narrower, while the piece on the far end looks shorter than does the piece at the end nearest to us. This drawing shows us what the base will look like, viewed from near one end, but it will not be of much help in telling us how to cut and join the pieces we need to make up this base.

Another pictorial drawing, the *isometric* view, as shown in *Figure 2*, also gives us an idea of how the finished base will look. It also distorts some of the details and dimensions of the object, but it can give us an accurate basis for scaling the major dimensions for making the welded iron base.

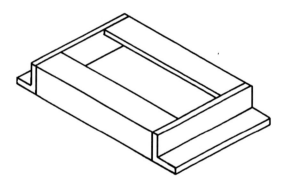

Figure 2 — Isometric drawing of the simple welded base

In the isometric drawing in *Figure 2*, the lines are laid out parallel to each other, at equal distances apart, and they show equal lengths. The width and length of the object are laid out to scale on sloped or inclined lines, which usually are at 30° to the horizontal base line. Height and depth are scaled on vertical lines, as shown in *Figure 2-A*.

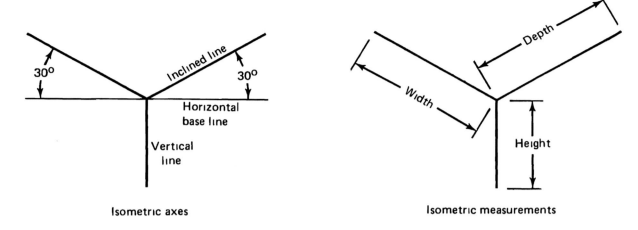

Isometric axes   Isometric measurements

Fig. 2-A — Angles used in isometric drawing

When we look at *Figure 2*, we see that it would be possible to measure the length and width of each leg and each end of the base, and the distances between them, fairly accurately. Looking at *Figure 2-B*, however, we find there is some distortion in this drawing. Distances A-D and B-C are equal; and so are lines A-C and D-B. The diagonal distances, A-B and D-C, however, are *not* equal on our drawing, even though we know they would be equal if the completed base has the square corners which we expect it to have.

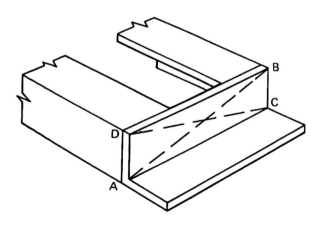

Fig. 2-B — Distortion of dimensions in isometric drawing

THE THREE-VIEW DRAWING

If we are going to build this simple welded base, or any other object, we are going to need drawings that will give us accurate dimensions and shapes and angles for all the parts of the object. We will need a drawing, or a set of drawings, that will let us see all of these details clearly and accurately, and in the correct relationship to each other.

Suppose that we could set our completed welded base up on blocks inside a large box which is constructed entirely of six sheets of clear plastic, as in *Figure 3*. The sides and ends of the base are parallel to the sides and ends· of the plastic box, and the top of the object is parallel to the top of the box. Now, we can walk around this box and look at our object from all four sides; we can look down at it from the top; and we can even crawl under the box and look *up* at the object if we want to see what it looks like from down there.

If we can imagine the picture we would get from each of these six observation points, we would see that each view tells us something important about the object — but that no one view tells us everything that we need to know in order to make the welded base.

3

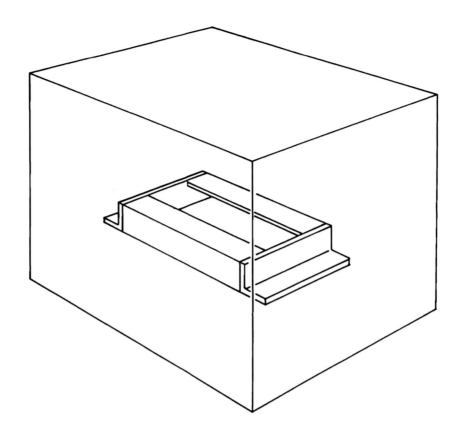

Fig. 3 — Welded base inside clear plastic box, viewed at an angle

Now, if we want to make drawings of what we see, we can use a grease pencil and draw right on our plastic box. Standing squarely in front of the box, we can make points or lines on the plastic exactly where we see them on the object inside the box. These marks would be placed on the plastic sheet at the precise point where an imaginary line, at right angles to the plastic sheet, and extended from the point or edge being viewed, meets the front of the box. Note that we would move our viewing eye to a new position for each point, so that the line-of-sight from the eye to the point being projected always is at right angles to the front surface of the box.

If we do this from the front of the box, then from the top, and again from the right side, we would get three different drawings of the object, projected onto these three sheets of plastic, as in *Figure 4.*

These three views are called *projected* views. If we remember that each line-of-sight must be at right angles to the surface of the box, we will have produced what is known as a "right angled projection of points." We can now use a Greek word, *orthographic,* which means *"right angled writing,"* to describe this method of drawing. This method of drawing is called *orthographic projection.*

4

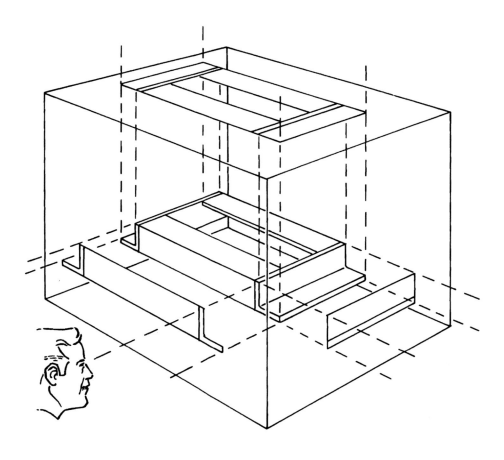

Fig. 4 — Line-of-sight projection of three views
of object to sides of the plastic box

By looking at all three projected views of our welded base we can check the relationship of a point in one view with a line in one or both of the other views. We can see that each detail on any one view also shows up in the other views, and that each view tells us something about the three-dimensional object itself that we would not get from any one view alone. Check this out in *Figure 4* by observing where each edge or corner appears in each view and compare your conclusions with your mental picture of the welded base. Do this carefully, until you are sure you understand just how each edge and corner of the object

shows up in the various views. Your ability to visualize these projections is the cornerstone for your ability to read shop drawings.

Since our drawing must be made on a flat sheet of paper, the three views must be shown in a way that will demonstrate the fact that they really are projected at right angles to each other. How can we do this on a flat sheet of paper? Suppose that the transparent sides and top of the plastic box were hinged together at the edges where they meet the front of the box. Now, if we swing the top and the right side around on their hinges, we

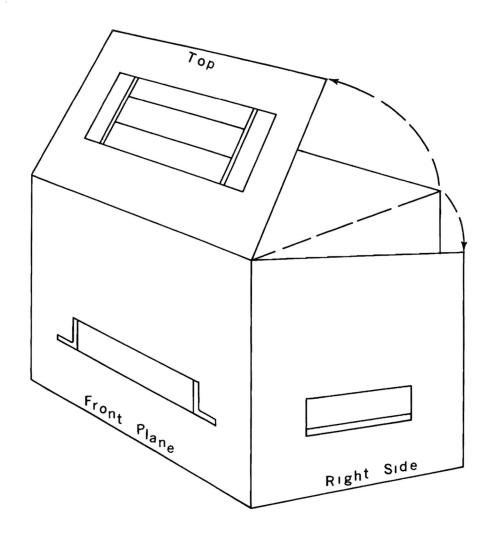

Fig. 5 — Hinged top and right side of plastic
box being swung toward plane of front of box

can bring them both into the same plane as the front of the box, as we are doing in *Figures 5 and 6.*

This change from a three-dimensional box to a flat sheet of paper will not be difficult to visualize if we remember to imagine the hinges on those front edges each time, and to swing the top and side of the box forward so that they are all on the same flat plane. The draftsman's next step is to draw the three views on his paper, just as they would appear if he had actually swung out the sides of our plastic box.

Looking at *Figure 6,* we can see that horizontal and vertical lines could be drawn which would connect the edges in the front view with edges in the side and top views. Can you also see that what appears as just a point in the front view becomes a line in the top view; that a point in the top view becomes a line in the front view; a point in the side view becomes a line in the front view, and so on?

After studying *Figure 6,* we can see very easily that the plastic box can be discarded, and that we could have drawn our three views directly on the paper without the box — pro-

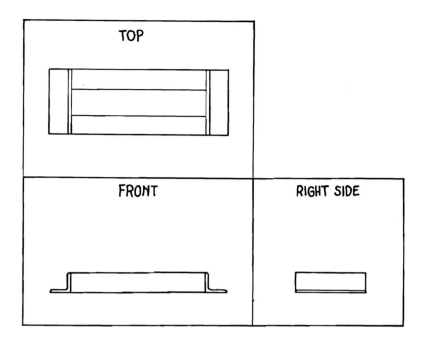

Fig. 6 — Front, top, and right side of plastic box all in same plane, showing three projected views of the welded base

vided that we placed them in the same relative positions and used the same rules of projection from one view to another. *Figure 7* shows our three-view orthographic projection without any plastic box.

Let's look now at a few examples of very simple projections, to better understand the method and learn how to read these projections.

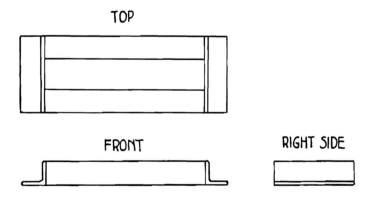

Fig. 7 — The three projected views of *Figure 6,* with plastic box removed, and the views moved closer together

In *Figures 8 to 10* we will look at points and lines, to see how they project from one view to another.

In *Figure 8* we have placed a single point inside a clear plastic cube or box. This is simply a dot suspended in space inside the cube; it has no dimensions. No matter where we stand to look at it, we see it only as a dot, in any view.

In *Figure 10* we have a line inside the box which is still in the horizontal plane (parallel to top and bottom) but whose left end is farther away from the observer than is the right end. It now appears in all three views, but will not show the same length in all three views; only the *top* view will show the true length of this particular line.

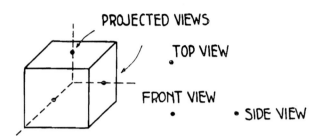

ORTHOGRAPHIC DRAWING

Fig. 8 — Point in center of plastic cube, observed from front, top and right side of the cube

When we look at *Figure 9* we see a line which has been placed in our box horizontal to the front and the top of the box. Remembering the principle that the line-of-sight for each point on an object is at right angles to the side of our plastic box through which we are viewing the object, we see that our line appears only as a single dot in the right side view. In front and top views we see the entire line.

PROJECTED VIEWS

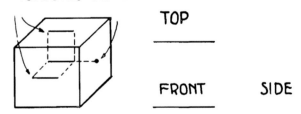

ORTHOGRAPHIC DRAWING

Fig. 9 — Line in center of cube, observed from three sides

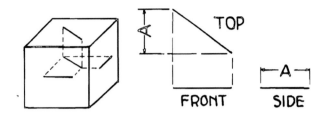

Fig. 10 — Three views of this line show it to be horizontal, but with left end further away from viewer by the distance A

Look back now at *Figures 6 and 7*, and project each point or line in any one view of the welded base into a point or line in the other two views. You are now *reading* this simple shop drawing.

Knowing that this base is fabricated from angle iron, we would know certain facts about the surfaces which are not visible to the eye from a particular view. But what if we did not know these facts already — how would the draftsmen help us to visualize thickness of the material, rounded corners, etc. which would not show up as we looked at the piece from the outside of the plastic box? He gives us this information about inside surfaces, edges, corners, etc. by using *hidden outline* lines. The *hidden* line is a series of *short dashes*, usually called a "dotted" line; the *solid* line is used to show all outlines *visible* to the observer in a particular view.

-------------------- hidden outline

————————— visible outline

Now, using both hidden and visible lines, we see in *Figure 11* what our base in *Figure 7* really would look like if we could see through the solid material it will be made of.

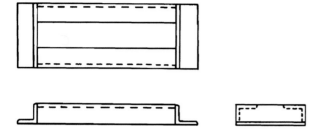

Fig. 11 — Orthographic drawing with dotted lines showing hidden edges of surfaces not visible from the various views

As we think further on the subject of giving complete information in an orthographic drawing, we see the need for more kinds of lines, to reveal certain kinds of details. For objects which are symmetrical about a center line or a plane (where one half of the piece is exactly the same shape and dimensions as the other), we need a *centerline:*

 - centerline

The centerline is always used to show the center of a hole or a cylinder; the center is the most important fact in drilling a hole, or in turning a shaft. *Figure 12* uses both dotted and center lines to describe the holes to be bored in this object. The piece will be bored part way through with a hole of one size, and then the rest of the way with a smaller hole.

To make or use this piece we need not only the shapes, both external and internal, but we also need all of the dimensions; these will be shown with the use of dimension lines which will be discussed a little later.

Figure 13 shows the dimension lines added to the front view of the welded base. The lines coming from the figure are called *extension* lines; they provide a place for the dimensions to be given clearly, without having them placed on the figure itself.

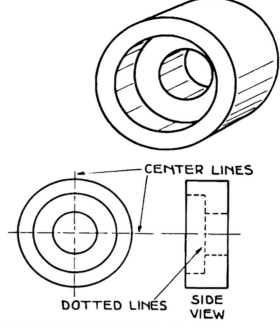

ORTHOGRAPHIC DRAWING

Fig. 12 — Counterbored collar. Only front and right side views are shown, since top view would be same as right side view. Dotted lines show hidden surfaces and edges.

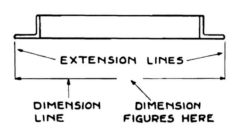

Fig. 13 — Front view of welded base shown with dimension lines added

It sometimes is important and helpful to show details of inner construction to show the object had been cut in two at some particular plane. A drawing is then made to show what the object would look like at that plane. A *cutting plane* line is used on the main drawing to show where the object is cut and the direction in which the observer is to look at the cut surface, as in *Figure 14.*

9

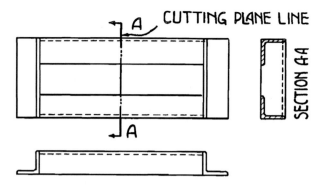

Fig. 14 — Welded base drawing with sectional view to show inner details

For some objects, which are uniform throughout their length, it is not necessary to make a complete drawing. The drawing can be shortened by omitting a part of this uniform section. This is indicated by the use of a *break* line, which usually is wavy or jagged. A pictorial outline may sometimes be used, as with the "broken" shaft in *Figure 15.*

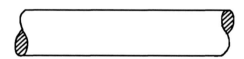

Fig. 15 — "Broken" shaft

Figure 15-A shows the use of a break line applied to our welded base. It might be used here if the base were to be a very long object and the amount of space available to illustrate it was limited.

"BREAK" LINE

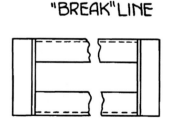

Fig. 15-A — Break line used on welded base drawing

ALPHABET OF LINES

We have now learned an alphabet of lines that are used to show various types of outlines and the way they intersect and relate to each other. Here they are in review:

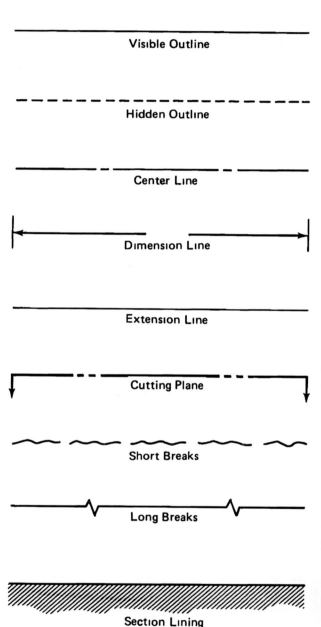

PRACTICE IN READING THREE-VIEW DRAWINGS

Now that we know some of the alphabet of lines and of shop drawings, let's try to actually read some of this new language. Look at each of the orthographic drawings in *Figures 16 to 19*, and try to read them — try to visualize for yourself just what the finished object will look like, either in its plastic box or out in the open by itself. Make a rough sketch of your own, in the space next to the three-view drawing, like a perspective or isometric drawing, to show what *you* think the object should look like. Then compare your sketches with the drawings in *Figures 16-A to 19-A*. Do the best you can with each one of these figures. This practice reading can be very important to you right now as you are learning to read this new language.

Learning to read by Sketching

USE THIS SPACE FOR YOUR SKETCH

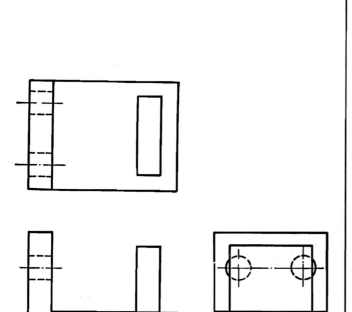

Fig. 16 — Degree gauge

Figures 16 and 16-A show a simple study of a degree gauge, with three main elements.

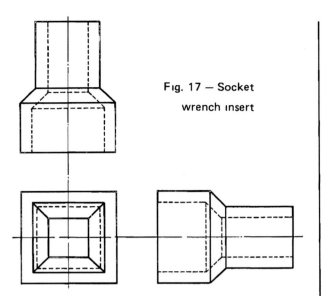

Fig. 17 — Socket
wrench insert

Figures 17 and 17-A are for an insert for a socket wrench. The isometric view shows us what the insert will look like, but does not give us the specific information we need to measure angles and the reductions of size. Only the orthographic, or three-view drawing gives us this information clearly.

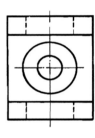

Fig. 18 — Bracket

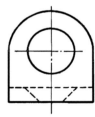
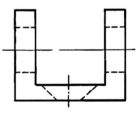

Figures 18 and 18-A show a simple bracket, with a countersunk hole in its base. Only the three-view drawing shows clearly the location and size of the hole and the angle of the countersink.

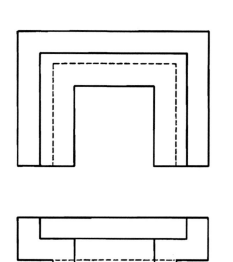

Figures 19 and 19-A show a special bracket which has parallel surfaces at several levels. The pictorial drawing shows us what it will look like, while the three-view drawing shows us exactly where these surfaces are in relation to each other.

Fig. 19 — Special bracket

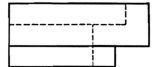

USE THIS SPACE FOR YOUR SKETCH

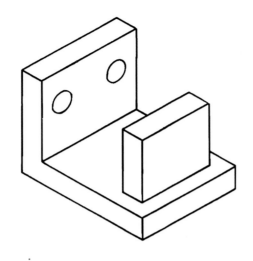

Fig. 16 — A

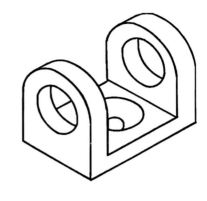

Fig. 18 — A

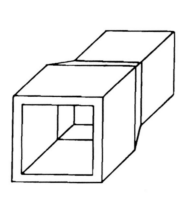

Fig. 17 — A

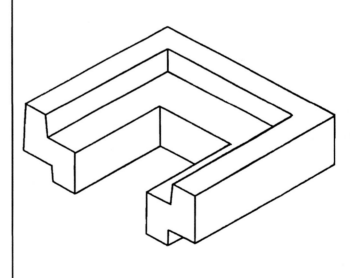

Fig. 19 — A

MORE READING PRACTICE

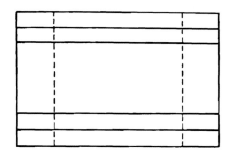

In *Figures 20 to 23* you will find several types of objects — some fairly simple, and some a little more complicated. Make a pictorial drawing for each one of these objects — a sketch of the part *as you see it*, as you read the three-view drawing. Study each drawing. Make your own sketch. Then compare your "reading" with the one given later.

Figures 20 and 20-A show a clamp plate with several levels and surfaces.

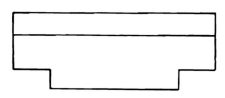 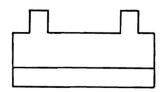

Fig 20 — Clamp plate — orthographic drawing

USE THIS SPACE FOR YOUR SKETCH

15

Figures 21 and 21-A show a lever for turning or controlling a shaft. Take a close look at the keyway shown in the front view, for locking the lever to the shaft, and see how this keyway is shown in the side view.

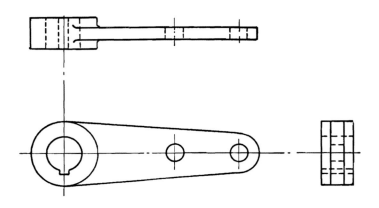

Fig. 21 — Lever

USE THIS SPACE FOR YOUR SKETCH

Figure 22 is a sheave housing. Study each line carefully before you make your pictorial drawings of the objects in both these figures, in the space at the right. Then compare your drawings with *Figures 22-A and 23-A*.

USE THIS PAGE FOR YOUR SKETCHES

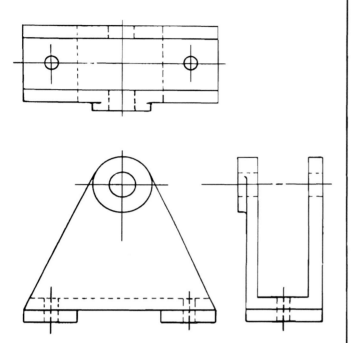

Fig. 22 — Sheave housing

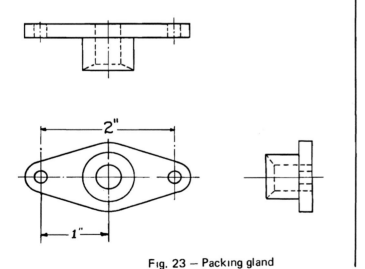

Fig. 23 — Packing gland

17

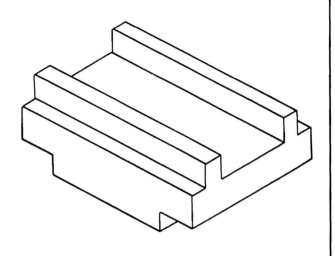

Fig. 20 — A

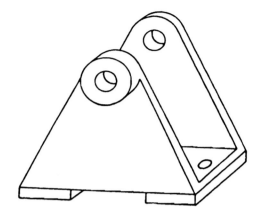

Fig 22 — A

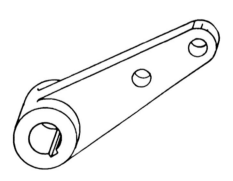

Fig. 21 — A

In *Figure 23-A* the picture drawing suggests that the center hole is countersunk, but does not give any specific information about it. The use of dotted lines, in *Figure 23*, however, clearly shows the details of this countersunk hole, in the top and right side views. The dash-dot lines in the front view give the machinist the exact locations of all three holes and the distances between their centers.

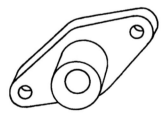

Fig. 23 — A

18

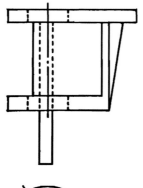

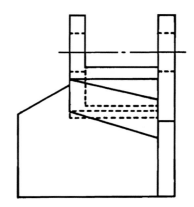

Figure 24 shows a very oddly formed bracket which requires careful inspection of its three orthographic views before we can visualize and draw the correct pictorial view, as shown in *Figure 24-A*.

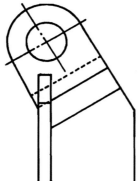

Fɪg. 24 — Angled bracket

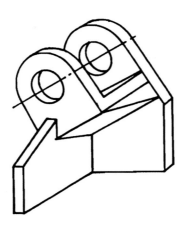

Fɪg. 24 — A

19

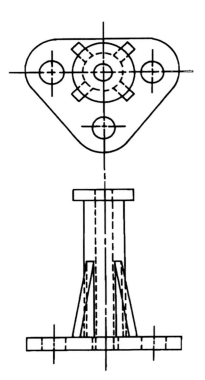
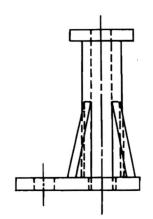

Figures 25 and 25-A show a rod support, with four fin-shaped braces. Of the three views in the orthographic drawing, only the top view gives a really good picture. But the front and side views are required to show us the remaining details.

Fig. 25 — Rod support

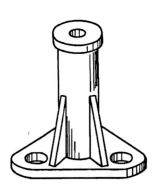

Fig. 25 — A

Figures 26, 26-A, 27 and 27-A show that it sometimes is necessary to use other views — left side, bottom, or perhaps even a rear view, to fully explain the object for the reader of the drawing.

Figure 26 is a good example of a drawing which gives information for machining. The left side view was used here to bring out details of that side as visible outline, instead of the hidden outline in which they appear in the front view.

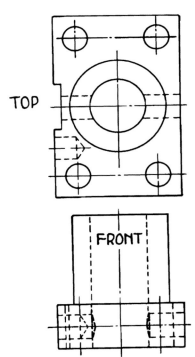

TOP

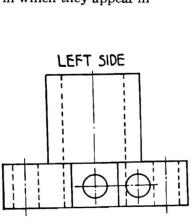

LEFT SIDE

FRONT

Fig. 26 — Jig fixture

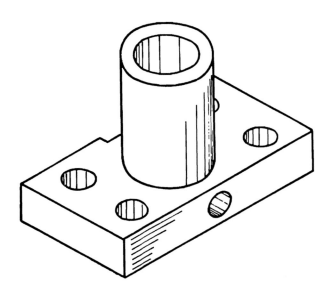

Fig. 26 — A

21

Figures 27 and 27-A show a support bearing which required both right and left side views to show it clearly. Neither of the side views alone would have given us a clear understanding of the details at the two ends of the piece.

The choice of views is a problem faced by the draftsman, who must present his subject as clearly as possible. As we see in this case, the left side view appears to the left of the front view, in a natural relationship to that view. If a bottom view is used, it will appear below the front view, just as it would show through the bottom of our clear plastic box.

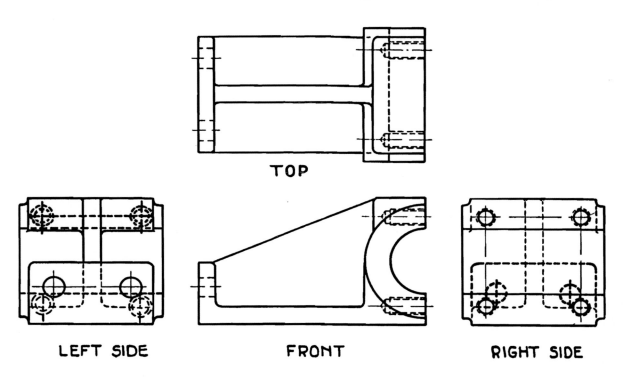

Fig. 27 — Support bearing

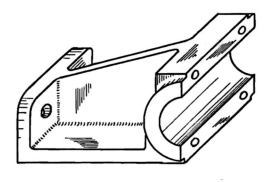

Fig. 27 — A

DIMENSION LINES

Another kind of line, which we have mentioned previously, is the *dimension* line, which tells us what the measurements of the object, and various parts of it, should be from point to point.

A shop drawing, especially one drawn to small scale, cannot be reproduced as a blueprint, or in any other of the modern methods of reproduction, with exact accuracy. There are many factors which interfere with such accuracy, including paper shrinkage, variations in setting of the camera or other device for enlargement or reduction, variations in chemical processing, etc. For these reasons, we cannot take measurements directly from the drawing with a rule or scale. We must use the dimensions which the draftsman has put on the drawing for us.

The dimension line, as shown in the Alphabet of Lines on page 10, includes a straight line, drawn rather lightly, with an arrowhead at each end, whose points just touch the *extension* lines coming from the object. The dimension line has a break in the middle, where the dimensions are inserted, in feet and inches or in centimeters and millimeters. Various methods of showing the dimensions are illustrated in *Figure 28*.

The point of the arrowhead may touch an extension line from a visible outline, a hidden outline, or a center line. The extension line also is drawn lighter than the outlines of the object; it does not actually touch the outline; and it is used *only* for indicating dimensions.

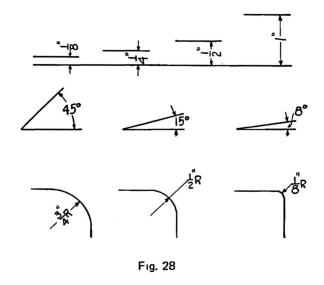

Fig. 28

The letter *R* indicates a Radius; the letter *D* a Diameter.

The dimension figures usually are placed so that they can be read from the bottom and from the right side, or right hand edge, of the drawing.

Figure 29 is our familiar welded base, with its dimensions added.

ALL necessary dimensions should be given on the drawing. The reader should not be required to make any calculations, since this practice could introduce errors.

Where a dimension must be maintained within certain limits, or *tolerances*, it is shown this way:

$$2000 \begin{array}{l} +.000 \\ -.002 \end{array} \quad \text{or} \quad 3.050 \begin{array}{l} +.002 \\ -.003 \end{array} \text{ etc.}$$

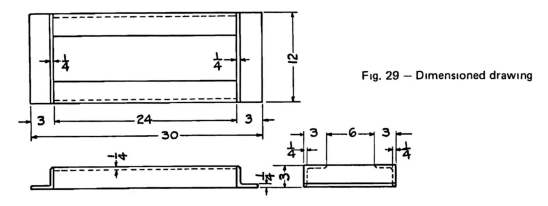

Fig. 29 — Dimensioned drawing

DRAWING TO SCALE

Many drawings obviously cannot be made to full size. For large objects, then, the shop drawing is made "to scale," with all details of the object shown in the proper relationships to each other, and in the proper proportions to each other, just as with a scale-model boat or airplane. Scale drawings may be made half-size, quarter-size, or to some other scale such as 1/4" to the foot as for floor plans, shop layouts, building sites, etc. The drawing usually will have a note indicating the scale used when the drawing was made, such as:

$$1" = 1"$$
$$1/4" = 1"$$
$$1/8" = 1"$$
$$1" = 1'$$
$$1" = 10'$$
etc.

In making sketches for your own use, you may use a wood or metal "scale" like the ones used by draftsmen. Scales are marked in feet and inches, or in centimeters, millimeters, etc., and in various reduction ratios. With such a scale, you can lay out the reduced dimension on paper simply by reading, on the

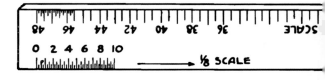

Fig. 30. Two Sides of a Commercial Scale.

scale, the full dimension taken from the object or planned for it. *Figure 30* shows a scale marked in four different ratios — full, half, quarter and eighth. If you want to mark out a dimension, or to check the *approximate* dimension on a shop drawing, use the edge of the scale that corresponds to the ratio of the drawing itself. *Figures 31 and 32* illustrate the use of other ratios on scaled drawings.

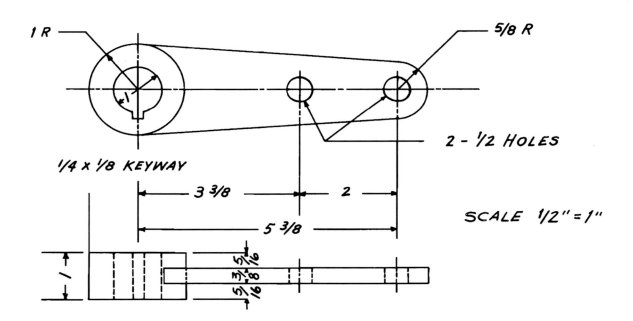

Fig. 31. Typical Scaled Drawing.

24

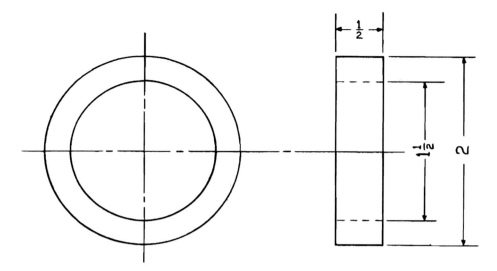

FULL SIZE   SCALE 1"= 1"

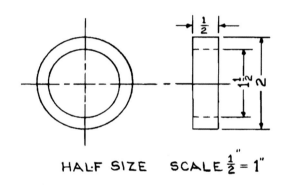

HALF SIZE   SCALE $\frac{1}{2}$" = 1"

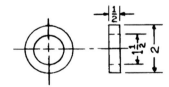

QUARTER SIZE SCALE $\frac{1}{4}$"= 1"

Fig. 32

AUXILIARY VIEWS

Every drawing should include enough views so that a clear idea of the object will be given to the reader or worker. The number and kind of views used will vary with the shape and details of the object to be drawn. In some cases, we will use *auxiliary* and/or broken views.

Some objects have a top or side surface which is not at right angles to the front surface. The exact shape and size of such a surface cannot be read easily from the views we have discussed up to this point. This is especially true when such a slanting part (which may be only a small part of a large machine) has curved edges and surfaces. Take a look at the angle brace, in the pictorial drawing in *Figure 33*.

If we put this brace into our clear plastic box, we find that the three usual views do *not* show definitely that the hole on the angled section is circular; nor do they show what size it is. To show these facts we need another view — one that is at right angles to the sloping surface. This will be an *auxiliary view*.

The auxiliary view, at right angles to the sloping surface, may be developed very easily. We can incline one side of our plastic box at the same angle as the sloping surface of the brace (in a plane parallel to the plane of the surface), and use our line-of-sight procedure to project the shape of the surface onto the plastic box, just as we have done before.

Figure 34 is a pictorial drawing of the plastic box, with part of the top slanted at the same angle as the sloping surface of the brace. Lines made with long dashes are extended, at right angles to the sloping surface, to project the corners of the surface onto the plastic box, thus creating our auxiliary view on that surface.

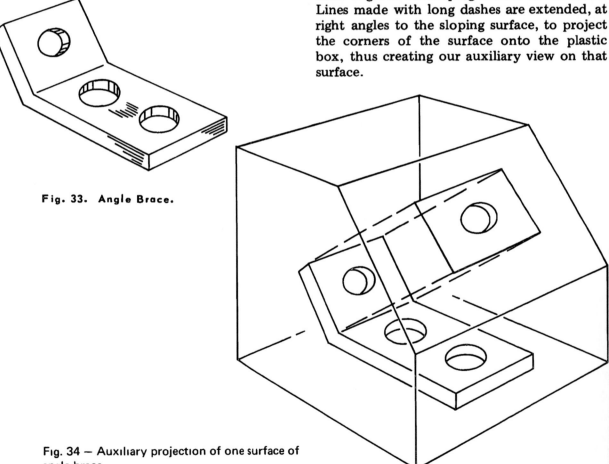

Fig. 33. Angle Brace.

Fig. 34 — Auxiliary projection of one surface of angle brace

26

Figure 35 shows this view as it would appear in a blueprint or shop drawing. Definite proof that the hole is circular is shown in this auxiliary view. Since trying to show the *entire* object in this auxiliary view would be very confusing, the view is cut or broken so that it includes *only* the sloping surface which needs the extra explanation.

TOP

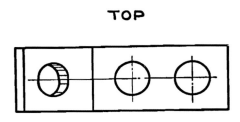

AUXILIARY VIEW

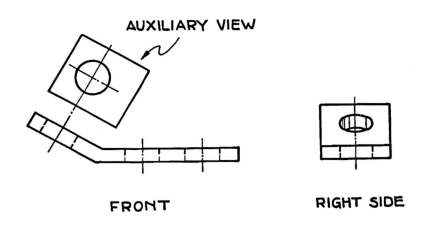

FRONT   RIGHT SIDE

Fig. 35 — Orthographic drawing of angle brace with auxiliary view

27

Figure 36 shows a bracket which requires an explanatory or auxiliary view to show the exact shape of one part — the angled section at the right end, in the right side view.

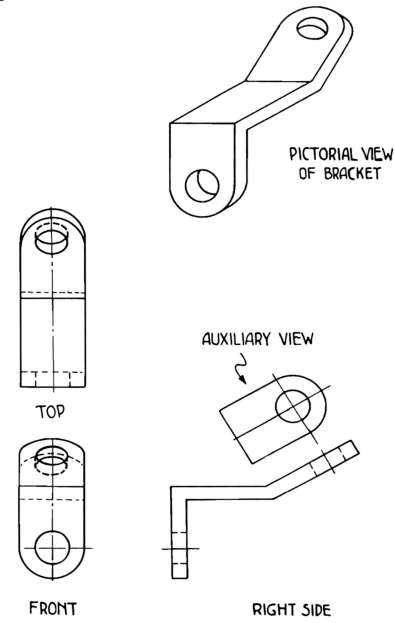

PICTORIAL VIEW
OF BRACKET

AUXILIARY VIEW

TOP

FRONT

RIGHT SIDE

Fig. 36 — Angle bracket

Figure 37 shows a slanting base which needs the definite dimension information contained in the auxiliary view to describe it completely for the person who is going to fabricate it.

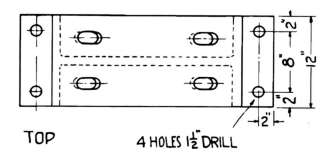

TOP

4 HOLES 1½" DRILL

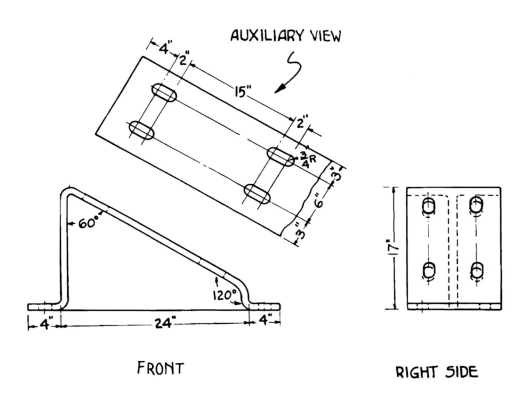

AUXILIARY VIEW

FRONT

RIGHT SIDE

Fig. 37 – Slanting base

SECTIONAL VIEWS

The exact shape of one part of an object — especially a smaller section in the center of the object — may be very difficult to illustrate because of the many confusing lines required in a conventional three-view drawing. A *section*, or *sectional view*, may then be added to show what the object would look like if a part of it had been cut away and removed. The cut surface is suggested on the drawing by cross-hatching or by slanted lines within the outline of the shape.

A section really is a picture drawing, used to visualize the shape at one particular place, on a plane cutting through the object at right angles to the surface of the drawing paper. This *cutting plane* is shown by a line through the conventional view, with arrows to show the direction of viewing (from the reader's eye) and letters, such as A-A, to identify it in the drawing. The section may be shown within the conventional view, as in *Figure 38*, or in a separate view, as in *Figures 39, 40 and 41*.

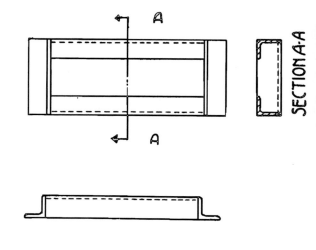

Fig. 39 — Welded base, with sectional view

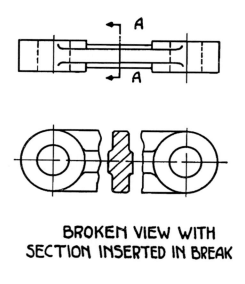

BROKEN VIEW WITH SECTION INSERTED IN BREAK

Fig. 38 — Bracket or brace, with sectional view

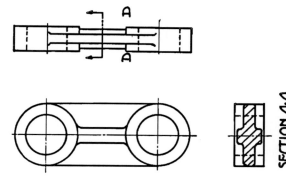

Fig. 40 — Same bracket, with sectional view

30

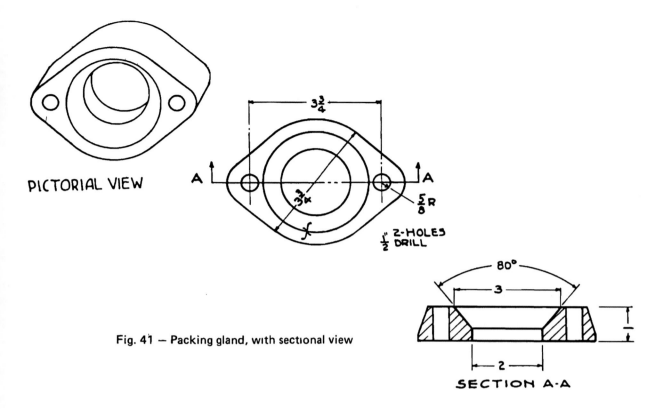

PICTORIAL VIEW

Fig. 41 — Packing gland, with sectional view

SECTION A-A

When a piece has the same dimensions over an extended portion of its length, a segment of that unchanging section can be cut away, and the ends moved closer together, either to save space on the drawing as in *Figures 42 and 43,* or to allow for insertion of the sectional view as in *Figure 38.* Two types of *break lines* are shown in these figures.

Machining instructions, such as *finish,* sometimes are given on the drawing, indicated by a small *f* on the surface requiring finishing, or with an arrow pointing to that surface, as shown in *figures 41 and 42.* In some cases, other instructions, such as *drill, tap* or *ream,* also are marked on the drawing to show what is to be done with certain specific holes laid out there.

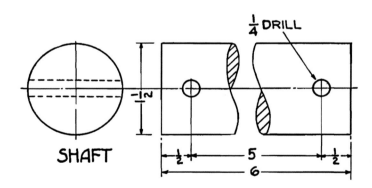

SHAFT

Fig. 42 — Shaft, with broken view

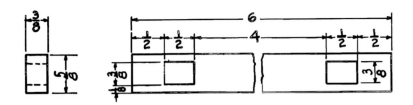

Fig. 43 — Slotted bar, with break, and sectional view

Screw threads are shown on shop drawings in many ways. In some cases, very accurate pictorial drawings are made of the thread. But in most cases, the thread is identified by a simple symbol, and a note is added to specify the type and size of the thread.

Figure 44 shows several typical illustrations of screw thread symbols — in direct outline form, as hidden outlines, and as sectional views.

SCREW THREAD SYMBOLS

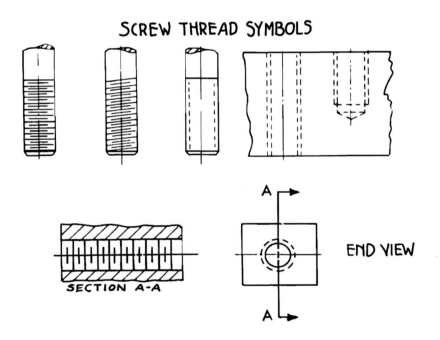

Fig. 44 — Screw threads in section

32

ISOMETRIC DRAWINGS IN USE

The construction details of the portion of our welded base shown in *Figure 45* are not difficult to understand. But the *appearance* of the finished piece may be a little more difficult to visualize from this drawing. The *isometric* drawing of the same object, in *Figure 45-A*, gives us a better idea of how it looks, and allows us to look for ways to improve its appearance. Addition of the small end-plates, as shown in *Figure 45-B*, improves the appearance of this assembly considerably.

The design, and eye-appeal, of many objects, both consumer items and industrial or machine parts, is very important in today's market. People want attractive equipment for home and recreational use. Industrial managers have found that production workers often are less dissatisfied with their jobs — and therefore tend to be more productive — if machines and equipment are neat and clean in design, instead of being ugly and unattractive. The isometric drawing is important to both the designer and the fabricator in visualizing the final appearance of the object.

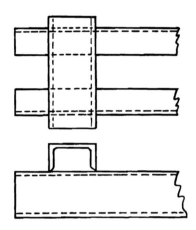

Fig. 45 — Orthographic views of part of welded base

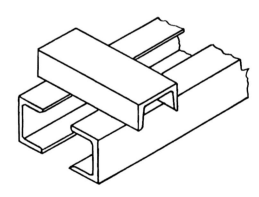

Fig. 45-A — Isometric view of same portions of welded base

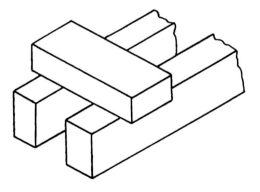

Fig. 45-B — Isometric view, with improved design

WELDING SYMBOLS

In Accordance With American Welding Society Standards

The painstaking care with which a designer develops his ideas is a trademark of his profession. The end product service requirements, such as operating temperatures and pressures, mechanical and physical properties and types of loading to which the purchaser will subject the product, are also considered complete. Each design detail must be carefully considered from an economic as well as an engineering and manufacturing standpoint before a designed structure or component is scheduled for production. In addition, the designer must be able to convey a complete knowledge of every design detail to the shop. Working shop drawings perform this function supplying the information necessary for low cost, accurate production.

Welding has assumed such importance in the fabricating field that it is absolutely essential to have some standard means of indicating on drawings the exact location, size, geometry and other pertinent information required for each weld.

The American Welding Society, recognizing this problem, has developed and adopted standard procedures for symbolically illustrating welds on engineering drawings. These procedures accommodate all processes and their application in the welding industry. Every weldor should become thoroughly familiar with these standard AWS welding symbols. Instructions for their use, as indicated herein, essentially conform to American Welding Society Standard AWS A2.0-68

ELEMENTS OF WELDING SYMBOLS

The American Welding Society welding symbol standard distinguishes between the terms weld symbol and welding symbol. The weld symbol is the ideograph used to indicate the desired type of weld. The assembled weld-

BASIC ARC WELDING SYMBOLS

LOCATION	Flash Or Upset	Groove					
	Square	Bevel	V	U	J	Flare Bevel	Flare V
Arrow-Side							
Other Side							
Both Sides							
No Arrow Side Or Other Side Significance	Not Used Except For Flash Or Upset Welds	Not Used	Not Used	Not Used	Not Used	Not Used	Not Used

Fig. 46. (Sheet 1)

34

ing symbol consists of eight elements, or as many of the eight elements as are necessary to completely describe a weld in terms of location, type, size and such other process data peculiar to individual shop specifications or requirements. These elements are:

1. Reference line
2. Basic weld symbols
3. Arrow
4. Dimensions and other data
5. Supplementary symbols
6. Finish symbols
7. Tail
8. Specification, process or other references

The information conveyed by the welding symbol is thus easily and accurately read, and long descriptive notes are not necessary.

REFERENCE LINE

The reference line of a welding symbol is that line depicted on a horizontal plane and joined to a tail and an arrow. The reference

SYMBOL	TYPE OF WELD
	Weld All Around (use with basic symbol)
	Field Weld (use with basic symbol)
(Basic)	Flush-Contour (use with basic symbol)
(Basic)	Convex Contour (use with basic symbol)
	Melt-Thru (use with basic symbol)

Fig 47. Supplementary Symbols.

BASIC ARC WELDING SYMBOLS

LOCATION	Flange		Fillet	Plug or Slot	Back or Backing	Melt-Thru	Surfacing
	Edge	Corner					
Arrow Side					GROOVE WELD SYMBOL		Not Used
Other-Side					GROOVE WELD SYMBOL		Not Used
Both Sides	Not Used	Not Used		Not Used	Not Used	Not Used	Not Used
No Arrow Side Or Other Side Significance	Not Used	Not Used	Not Used	Not Used	Not Used	Not Used	

Fig. 46 (Sheet 2)

35

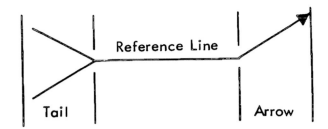

line, which is the basis of each simplified symbol, provides for the orientation and standard location of the elements of a welding symbol.

The position of the tail and arrow may be reversed but the elements of the symbol are always in the same position on the reference line.

BASIC WELD SYMBOLS

The basic weld symbols and the supplementary weld symbols are shown in Figures 46 and 47.

For more information on weld symbols see page 186.

The basic groove, plug, slot and flange weld symbols are used to show the approximate outline of the joint contour as prepared for welding.

The back or backing weld symbol is used to show a bead-type back or backing weld for single-groove welds.

The melt-thru weld symbol is used when at least 100 percent penetration of the weld through the material is required in welds made from one side only.

The surfacing weld symbol is used to show a surface built up by single- or multiple-pass surfacing welds, such as for hard-facing, or for building up a worn surface.

The flange welding symbols are used to show joints in light gage metal made by flaring or flanging the edges to be joined.

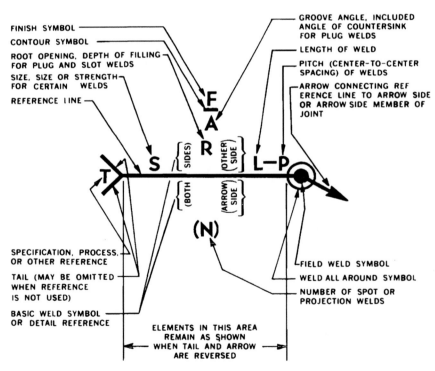

Fig. 48. Standard Location of Elements of a Welding Symbol.

Fillet, bevel groove, J-groove, flare-bevel groove and corner flange symbols are always shown with the perpendicular leg to the left:

When joints have more than one weld, both symbols are shown:

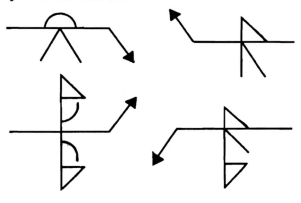

THE ARROW AND ITS LOCATION SIGNIFICANCE

To show the location of a weld, an arrow is drawn with the head pointing directly to the joint where the weld is to be made.

In the past, the use of the words "far side" and "near side" has caused confusion, since joints shown in section have all welds equally distant from the reader and the words "near" and "far" are meaningless. In accordance with the current standard for welding symbols, the joint is always the basis of reference. The placement of the weld symbol, which indicates the welding of any joint can, therefore, be used to indicate the "arrow side" of the joint. Accordingly, the words "arrow side," "other side" and "both sides" are used in this discussion to locate the weld with respect to the joint.

In the case of fillet, groove, and flange welding symbols, the arrow connects the welding symbol reference line to one side of the joint, and this side is considered the "arrow side" of the joint. The side opposite the "arrow side" of the joint is considered the "other side" of the joint.

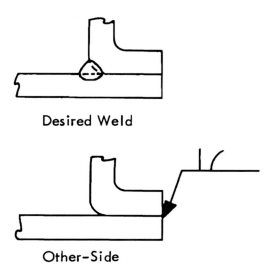

Desired Weld

Other-Side

Flare Bevel Groove Welding Symbol

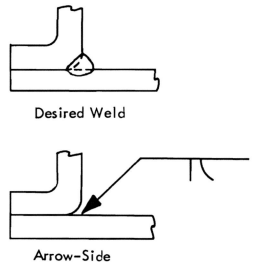

Desired Weld

Arrow-Side

Flare Bevel Groove Welding Symbol

In the case of plug or slot symbols, the arrow connects the welding symbol reference line to the outer surface of one of the members of the joint at the centerline of the desired weld. The member to which the arrow points is considered the "arrow side" member. The other member of the joint is considered the "other side" member.

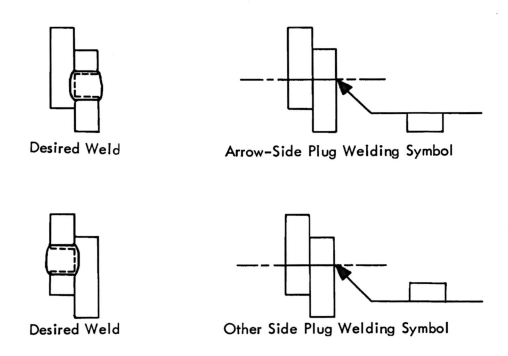

Desired Weld

Arrow-Side Plug Welding Symbol

Desired Weld

Other Side Plug Welding Symbol

When a joint is depicted by a single line on the drawing, and the arrow of a welding symbol is directed to this line, the "arrow side" of the joint is considered to be the near side of the joint in accordance with the usual conventions of blueprint reading.

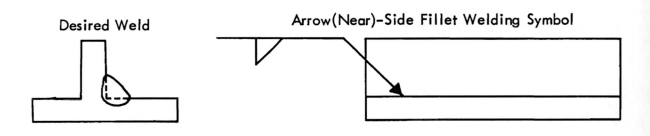

Desired Weld

Arrow(Near)-Side Fillet Welding Symbol

When a joint is depicted as an area parallel to the plane of projection on a drawing, and the arrow of a welding symbol is directed to that area, the "arrow side" member of the joint is considered to be the near member of the joint in accordance with the usual conventions of blueprint reading.

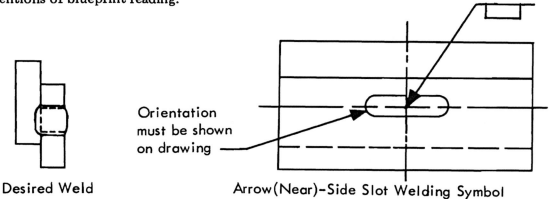

Desired Weld

Orientation must be shown on drawing —

Arrow(Near)-Side Slot Welding Symbol

Welds on the arrow side of the joint are shown by placing the weld symbol on the side of the reference line toward the reader, thus:

Welds on the other side of the joint are shown by placing the weld symbol on the side of the reference line away from the reader, thus:

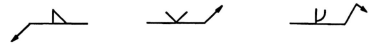

Welds on both sides of the joint are shown by placing weld symbols on both sides of the reference line, toward and away from the reader, thus:

Further illustration of this subject is found on page 65.

DIMENSIONS AND OTHER DATA

The dimensions shown in a welding symbol include size, groove angle, root opening, length of weld, pitch (center-to-center spacing) of welds, depth of filling of plug or slot welds, and included angle of countersink for plug welds. One or more of these may be specified, depending upon the type of joint and instruction required.

When welds on both sides of a joint have the same dimensions, one or both may be dimensioned on the welding symbol. When the welds differ in dimensions, both are dimensioned on the welding symbol.

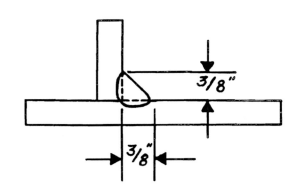

The size of a fillet weld is determined by the length of its shortest leg.

This dimension is shown to the left of the weld symbol on the same side of the reference line.

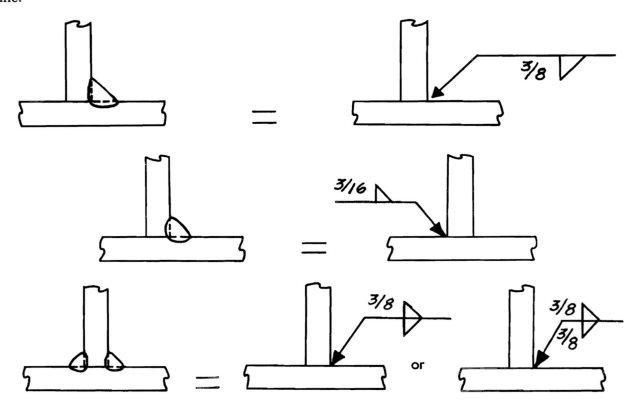

When the fillet welds differ in size, both are dimensioned.

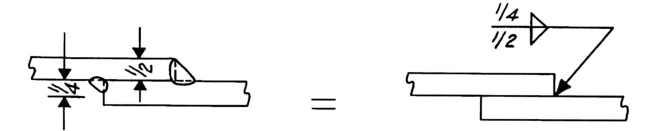

Further illustrations of fillet welding symbols can be found on page 68.

The size of a groove weld is the joint penetration (the depth of chamfering plus the root penetration when specified).

When root penetration is *not* specified:

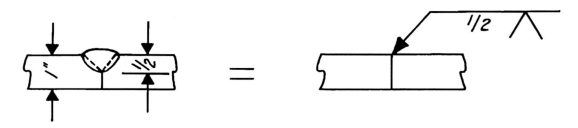

When root penetration *is* specified:

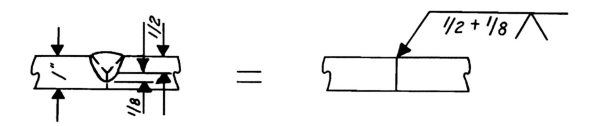

The size of a groove is shown to the left of the weld symbol. The arrow points to plate to be beveled when single bevel is specified. Groove dimension is shown when:

(1) The groove weld extends only partly through the parts being joined, thus:

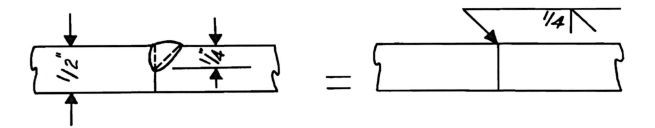

(2) The root penetration is specified in addition to the depth of chamfer, thus:

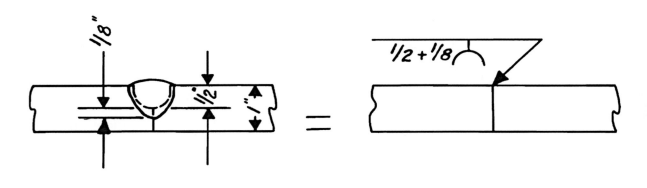

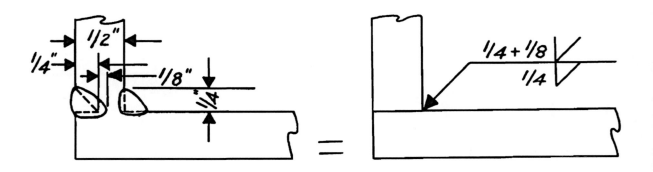

The dimension is not shown when:

(1) The single groove weld extends completely through the parts being joined. If 100 percent penetration is desired, either the melt-thru or back weld symbol is added, thus:

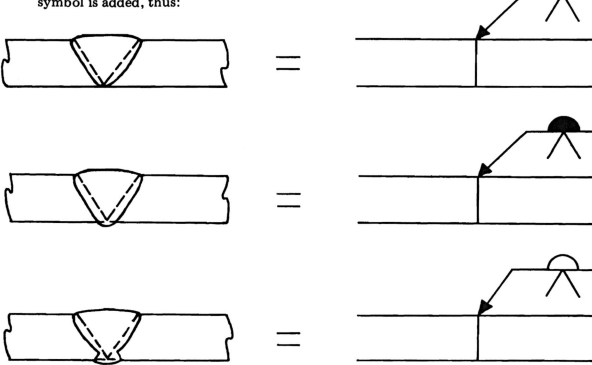

(2) Both sides of a double groove weld are the same and the weld extends completely through the parts being joined, thus:

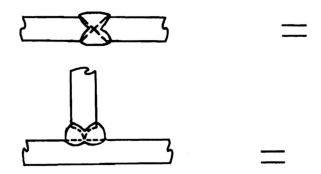

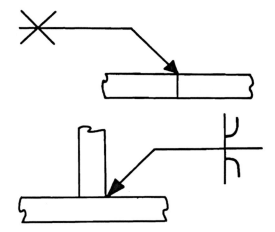

43

The size of a flare-groove weld is considered to extend only to the tangent points of the members:

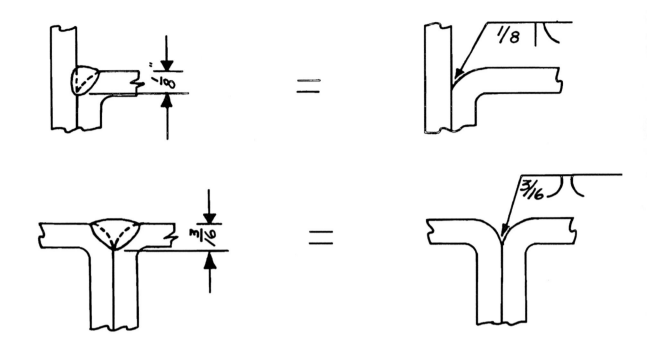

For flange welds, the radius and height above the point of tangency are shown as well as the size. The radius and height dimensions are separated by a plus mark.

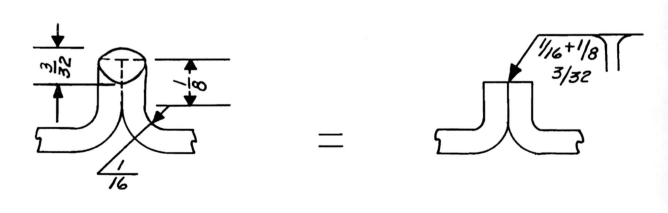

The size of a surfacing weld is shown to the left of the weld symbol and indicates the minimum height of the build-up. (The length and width of surface to be covered is shown by specific dimensions on the drawing.)

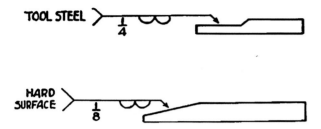

Groove angles and root openings, if in accordance with established shop standards, are not shown on the welding symbol. If not in accordance with shop standards, they are shown as illustrated on pages 55 through 64 and in Figure 48.

Length and pitch (center-to-center spacing) of welds are shown in the symbol as illustrated in Figures 53 and 54. When the length of weld is not given, the symbols apply between abrupt changes in the direction of welding, except when the weld-all-around symbol is used.

SUPPLEMENTARY SYMBOLS WELD

The weld-all-around symbol is used to show a weld which extends completely around a joint. Its use is illustrated in Figures 47 and 48.

The field weld symbol is used to show welds not made in the shop or place of initial construction.

SURFACE CONTOUR AND FINISH OF WELDS

Welds that are to be welded approximately flat-faced, without recourse to any method of finishing, are shown by adding the flush-contour symbol to the weld symbol, observing the usual location significance, thus:

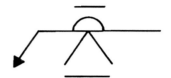

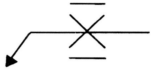

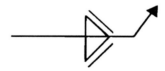

Where normal build-up from standard welding procedures is acceptable, the contour symbol is omitted.

Welds that are to be made flat-faced by mechanical means are shown by adding both the flush-contour symbol and the user's standard finish symbol* to the weld symbol, observing the usual location significance, thus:

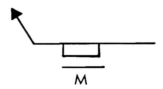

45

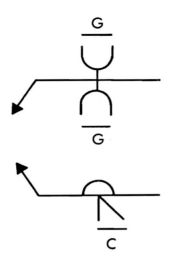

INDUSTRIAL EXAMPLES OF WELDMENTS

The use of welded steel design to improve machine performance and reduce manufacturing costs is as extensive as the creativeness of designers and engineers. The draftsman should be aware of the thinking that must go into a new product or redesign.

The following case histories present problems such as vibration, impact appearance, machining and other common difficulties that might be encountered. Detailed analysis and calculations are omitted to make the material more easily understood.

Welds that are to be mechanically finished to a convex contour, are shown by adding both the convex-contour symbol and the user's standard finish symbol* to the weld symbol observing the usual location significance, thus:

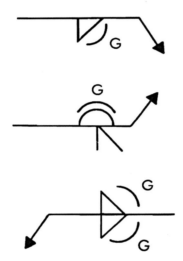

TAIL OF ARROW

In the tail of the welding symbol is placed the specification or process, or any special information as to shop practice or procedure.

DESIGN "FROM SCRATCH" TAKES
EXCESS COST FROM PRESS BRAKE BENDING

A.L. Wilson, Jr.
American Laundry Machy. Ind.
67-MD-23

Through routine cost analysis, it was learned that high labor costs for some of our better selling products resulted from the high cost of operating one press brake machine. Here, as many as five men (Figure 1) were required to make three housing wraps (Figure 2).

Observation of the bending operations at this machine indicated several inefficiencies. First, the material weight of the part was greater than could be handled by a normal press brake team of two men. Second, the longer sheets whipped upward while the first 90⁰ bend was being made. Third, the extra men served only to feed the heavier sheet, guild it into location against the stops, and retrieve the sheet after the bend.

First, attempts at correction met with no measurable success. Roller tables were set up to feed the sheet. This move looked promising, but on retrieval of the sheet from the braking die, the roller table got in the way of the men sliding the sheet out of the brake.

Hoists were put on the "tail" of the sheet to hold the end and lower it after the bending. This eliminated need for one man but increased operation time by 40%. The savings were negative. A commercial counterbalancing device was investigated, but this device would require another operator or a slowup of the operation if a two-man team were used. Payback would have been beyond our maximum for equipment of this type.

The final conclusion from these experiments was that our manufacturing method was incorrect.

The Solution to the Problem

The reasoning toward the eventual solution of the problem developed as follows:

1. The sheet should be mechanically supported to eliminate men handling the weight.
2. Sheet weight had to be controlled 100% of the operating time.
3. Unloading the machine should require no more help than the bending operation.

Two methods changes appeared possible. The first was the possible use of a machine known as a "Tangent Wing Bender," and the second was to use a vertical bending plane instead of a horizontal bending plane.

Investigation revealed that there were no standard "Tangent Wing Benders" that would handle our gage of metal with the varying bend configurations.

The second approach was to look for a source of a vertical press brake and use a suspensory device to hold the sheet. Four U.S. and one European sources were investigated with unrewarding results. The decision was made to build our own machine tool, a vertical press brake.

Figure 1 — As many as five men were required to handle the sheet.

Figure 2 — Three housing wraps, the bending of which required excessive labor.

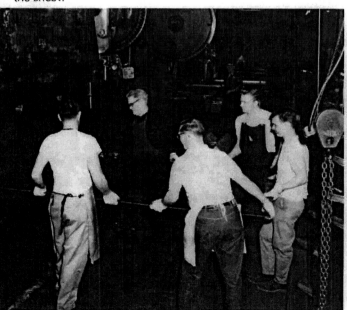

Design Criteria

The design criteria for the new machine tool were as follows:

1. The capacity of the machine should be at least 150 tons.

2. The sheet width-handling ability had to be at least 80 inches.

Figure 3 — A working model of the proposed bending machine.

Figure 4 — Sheet supports on the model were changed to the swing type after the original arrangement proved unsuccessful.

3. The machine should accept conventional press brake dies.

4. The machine should be able to bend all of our required shapes with a maximum of two men — an operator and a helper.

5. The machine should be designed in such a way that it could be assembled and disassembled at will and moved within our facility or to other facilities.

6. The machine would probably be "one of a kind." This precluded the use of castings and outside foundry work.

7. The bending force of the machine should be a controllable variable, as should the bending speed. The reason for this is that good quality and accuracy require full control of the machine tool.

The Working Model

Having no experience in the building of press brakes, we made sketches of various ideas, evolved a plan, and built a one-quarter scale model of the machine we envisioned.

Figure 3 shows the model from the "bending" side. The storage rack on the left holds the presheared sheets on edge, ready to be lifted from their support ledge. The jib boom with trolley will support the sheet in its movement from the rack to the bending die and in relocation for the subsequent bend. Note the bending cylinders (A) within the main column.

Figure 4 shows the die opening (A) and sheet stops (B). Control panel (C) is functional, but atypical. Sheet supports (D) were altered to swing type after "drag" on the working model proved unsuccessful.

Figure 5 — Rear view of the model.

Figure 5 shows the rear view of the model. The two sprockets with hand wheels (A) are chained die-gap adjustments. The pneumatic cylinder-hydraulic cylinder arrangement on the left (B) is the means for getting the hydraulic pressure to produce the bending force.

The Machine Tool

After the scale model was examined, tested, and modified, we began an investigation to determine stresses, final sizes, availability of components, and costs. The column and male die support sizes were mathematically calculated for depth. Figure 6 shows the column under construction. The finished weight of this component is 3700 pounds. Overall dimensions are 36" deep (front to back), 36" wide, and 80-3/4" high. Sides are 1-3/4" plate, bottom and top are 2" plate, and the back plate is 3" thick.

Figure 7 shows the rear of the machine in early stages of assembly, and Figure 8 the front view. Figure 9 shows the rear of the finished machine. Length of the base is 151", width is 82" (not including operator's platform), and the overall height is 108". Identified in this photo are the air-hydraulic actuators (A), hydraulic reservoirs (B), die-gap adjustment hand wheel (C), and accessory valving and piping (D).

Figure 7 — Rear of the machine during early stages of assembly.

Figure 8 — The front of the machine during assembly

Figure 6 — The column during fabrication.

Figure 9 — Rear of the finished machine.

Figure 10 — Front of the finished machine.

Figure 11 — Rear of the machine, with the operator removing bent sheet.

Figure 12 — The control panel.

are the female-die carriage-support bearing (C), the hydraulic cylinders (E), and the main column (F).

Results

The project presented many challenging problems. The most significant achievement was the simplicity developed in the end product.

Looking at the photographs, one might visualize many complications. They were, however, quite few. The drawings were all simple sketches made on 8-1/2" x 11" ruled paper.

Practically every piece of the machine had welded joints. Lap and butt joints predominated. Joints capable of disassembly were used only where wear might require part replacement, adjustment might be required, or disassembly might be necessary for machine relocation or major maintenance. A majority of welded joints assured the desired rigidity.

The completed machine performs as expected. It produces precise bends and requires but two men for its operation. On many parts, it saves well over 70% the cost of bending by the prior machine.

Figure 10 shows the front of the finished machine. Illustrated here are the male die support (F) made of 7" plate, the sheet support wings (B), pneumatic cylinder that produces wing motion (G), sheet working stops (C), and support hoist with jib boom (D).

Figure 11 shows the rear of the machine with the operator removing the bent sheet (A) from the press. The sheet material on rack (B) is raw stock awaiting bending. The control panel and gauges are indicated (C).

Figure 12 shows the control panel (A). Manipulating the switches controls sheet working stops (B) to permit the sheet to position and be bent at the proper line. Also shown

DECISIONS IN ABRASIVE MACHINING

Ronald S. Walker
Moorhead State College
67-MD-32

Abrasive belt machining seemed to be the solution to the need for versatility in working with a variety of different sizes, shapes, and types of metals as well as making possible a desirable surface finish. A rubber contact wheel could be used to furnish the resilient qualities needed in deburring and finishing. A platen could be incorporated to afford grinding of flat surfaces and squaring up stock.

Standard abrasive belt sizes were checked and a 2-1/2 x 48 inch size was chosen to fulfill the requirements of size portability. Welded steel fabrication was decided upon to keep initial tooling costs of manufacture to a minimum. Selection of materials was based on standard shapes and sizes readily available and feasibility of being shear cut and punched.

Hot rolled steel plate of 3/8" thickness was chosen for the frame base since this thickness made possible tapping and bolting of the motor and fixtures as well as being able to weld parts to it without danger of distortion. A size of 8" x 24" worked well from the standpoint of ease of shearing and no waste from stock sizes of 72" x 120" or 48" x 96" or 8" wide flat.

Angles 3" x 3" x 3/16" were chosen for the upright pieces and platen. These provided the necessary rigidity, maintained simplicity of fabrication, and could be shaped by shearing to provide satisfactory aesthetic design.

All holes can either be punched or drilled and threaded holes can be tapped on either a single or multiple spindle tapper.

The welding can be accomplished by the use of production locating jigs. The electrode decided upon and used was a 1/8" E6013 operated at 130 amps. The frame welds are inside corner 1/4 inch fillets 1/2 inch long spaced at one inch intervals. The upright angles that are welded to the plate are welded only on the inside so that contracting weld forces will be controlled by the opposite leg of the angle resulting in the angle being pulled down rather than to the side which would destroy squareness.

The platen is adjustable up and down for proper alignment with the belt. Tracking of the belt is accomplished by pivoting the idler pulley with the stop screw positioned

Figure 1

Figure 2

against the upright leg. Belt tightness is adjusted by positioning the motor

The pulleys used are aluminum castings which are very easy to machine The idler is machined with a two degree angle to the center for belt tracking The casting is bored for two double sealed ball bearings which are pressed into place The machining is accomplished by chucking in a lathe twice. Each time the casting is in the chuck, one half is machined to proper angle and a bearing hole is bored.

The drive pulley is machined flat and a half inch hole drilled for the arbor mount. Four layers of neoprene rubber are bonded to the pulley with industrial adhesive. The pulley is then ground on a cylindrical grinder between centers using a silicon carbide wheel and water coolant

After final machining both pulleys are balanced to insure smooth running

The finish chosen for the machine was a synthetic enamel in a rich blue It is a three dimensional hammertone industrial finish that covers well with one coat The finish is

applied by spraying and is dry enough to handle in fifteen minutes. The motors may be painted to match which does add considerably to the appearance of the machine. No masking is required in finishing the machine since the only parts not painted are the pulleys. These are assembled after finishing

The completed machine weighs fifty-five pounds which meets the requirements in portability. The flat base permits use on any bench with or without bolting down. The positioning of the drive pulley and platen on the left side of the machine permits working either from the side or front of the machine and seems easiest for a right handed person Long stock can be worked by running up and over either the drive wheel or the platen since there are no obstructions.

Abrasive belts in the 2-1/2 x 48 inch size are readily available. The belts used most satisfactorily are cloth backed, resin bonded in grits from 36 to 100.

The machine works well for sharpening tools, deburring, shaping, finishing of forged tools, shaping parts for machine

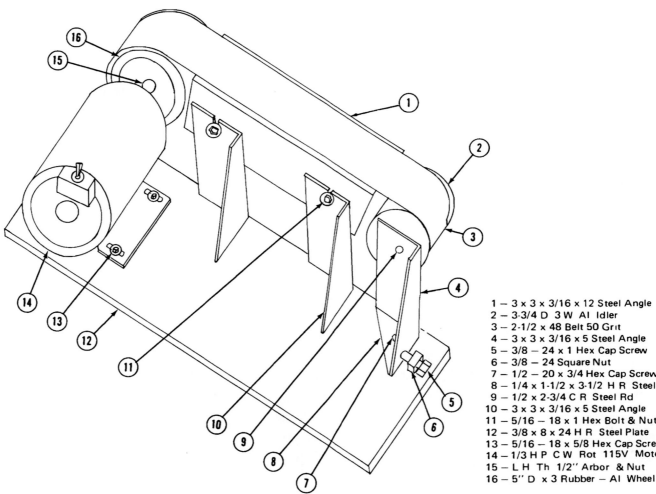

1 — 3 x 3 x 3/16 x 12 Steel Angle
2 — 3-3/4 D 3 W Al Idler
3 — 2-1/2 x 48 Belt 50 Grit
4 — 3 x 3 x 3/16 x 5 Steel Angle
5 — 3/8 — 24 x 1 Hex Cap Screw
6 — 3/8 — 24 Square Nut
7 — 1/2 — 20 x 3/4 Hex Cap Screw
8 — 1/4 x 1-1/2 x 3-1/2 H R Steel
9 — 1/2 x 2-3/4 C R Steel Rd
10 — 3 x 3 x 3/16 x 5 Steel Angle
11 — 5/16 — 18 x 1 Hex Bolt & Nut
12 — 3/8 x 8 x 24 H R Steel Plate
13 — 5/16 — 18 x 5/8 Hex Cap Screws
14 — 1/3 H P C W Rot 115V Motor
15 — L H Th 1/2" Arbor & Nut
16 — 5" D x 3 Rubber — Al Wheel

Figure 3 — Abrasive Belt Grinder Machine

and welding jigs, glass and ceramic edge finishing, rust, scale, and paint removal.

Welded steel is used for all parts in the fabrication of this machine with the exception of: the motor, drive arbor, and the two pulleys. All welded fabricated parts can be production sheared and punched. Assembly for welding is accomplished in production jigs.

The design of this machine has been tested for the past 18 months with various sizes of pulleys and types of rubber contact wheels. A grit 50 belt seems to be the most preferred for general work. The motor size seems to be satisfactory. The overall operation of the machine seems to be efficient and free from trouble.

Figure 4

53

NOTE: The next few pages are devoted to cross section views of various joints, and the symbol is shown with the joint it represents. Since the available combinations are numerous, not all the possible joints are shown. The square groove butt joint — with and without root openings — is completely covered, as is the single and double V groove joint. The included angle in the groove joint examples was chosen for illustration purposes only. If the included angle and also the root opening is standard for a particular shop, it may be omitted from the welding symbol. Since shop standards differ, these, as well as any other omitted dimensions, must be obtained from the proper plant authority.

For standardization and easy reference, letters are used in the following cross section views to represent specific dimensions:

P — Depth of Penetration
C — Depth of chamfer
θ — Included bevel or groove angle
r — Groove radius
R — Root opening
L — Root face or land
T — Weld Throat
W — Weld Size

* Finish symbols used herein indicate the method of finishing (C = chipping, G = grinding, M = machining) and not the degree of finish.

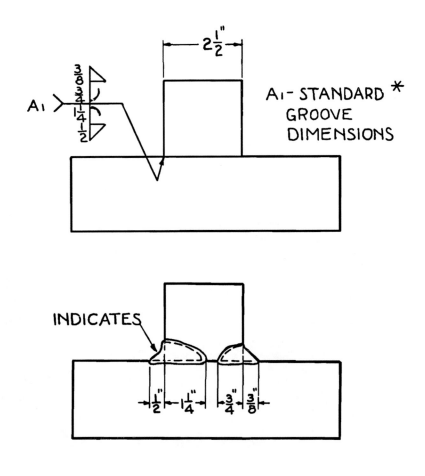

A₁- STANDARD *
GROOVE
DIMENSIONS

INDICATES

*Standard in the particular shop for which this drawing was prepared.

BUTT WELDS

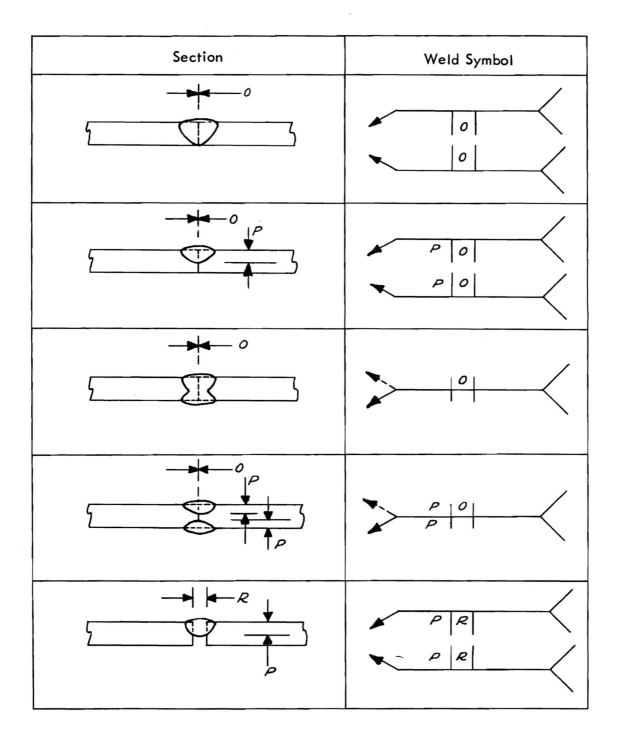

Section	Weld Symbol

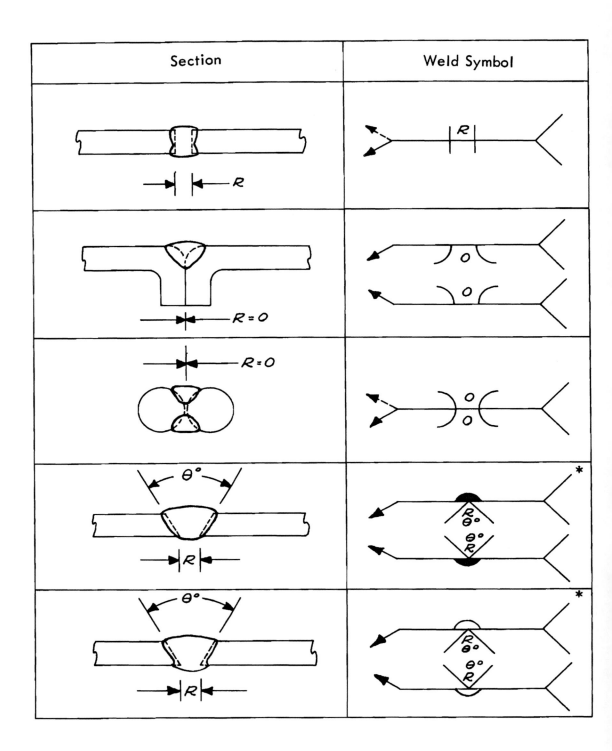

Section	Weld Symbol

*Root, opening and angle may be omitted if they are user's standard. See note on page 53.

Section	Weld Symbol

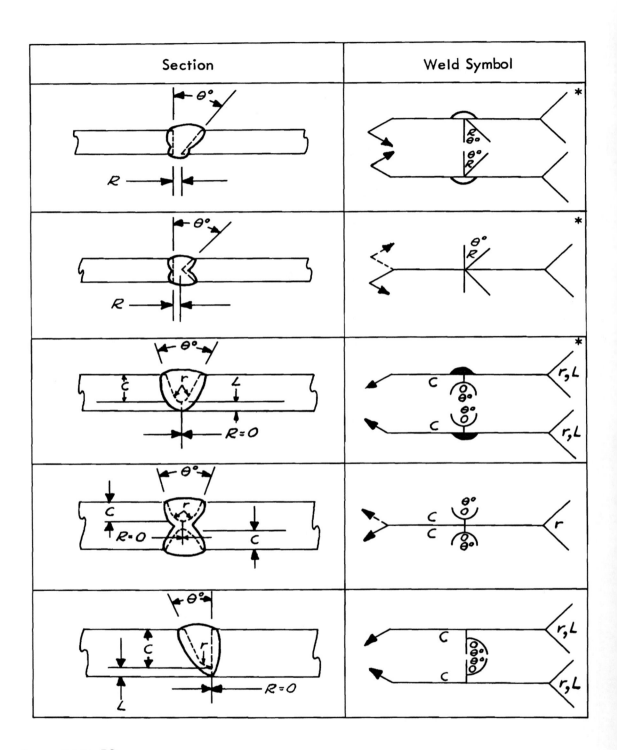

Section	Weld Symbol

*See note on page 53.

NOTE: In groove joints the root face (land) dimension (L) is sometimes specified rather than chamfer (C).

CORNER JOINTS

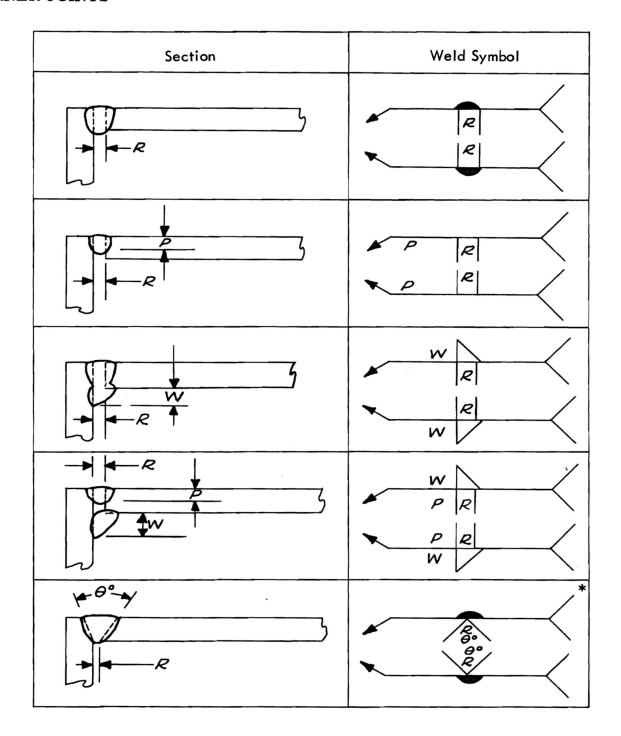

Section	Weld Symbol

*See note on page 53.

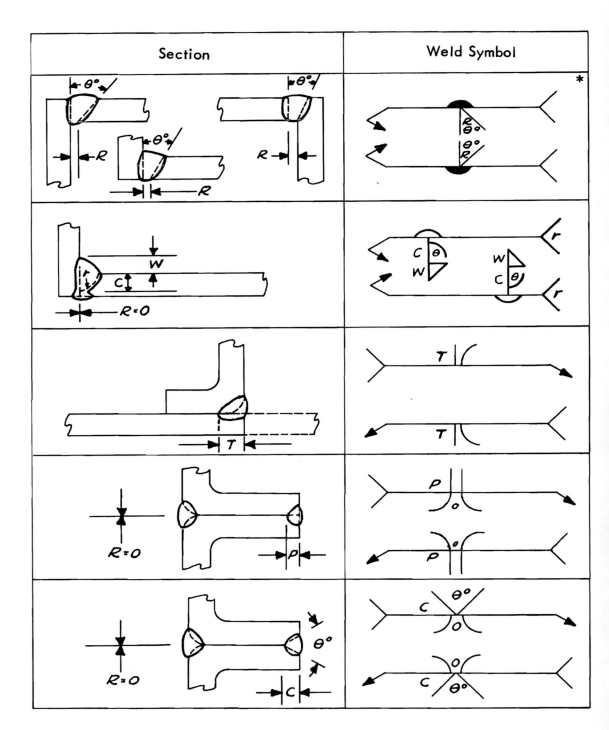

Section	Weld Symbol

*See note on page 53.

EDGE JOINTS—LIGHT GAUGE METAL

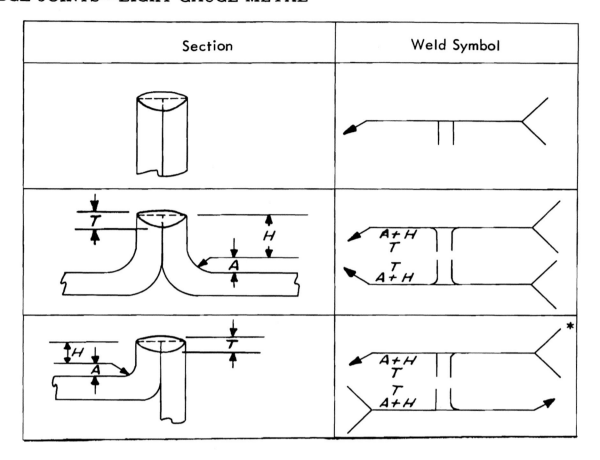

Section	Weld Symbol

LAP JOINT

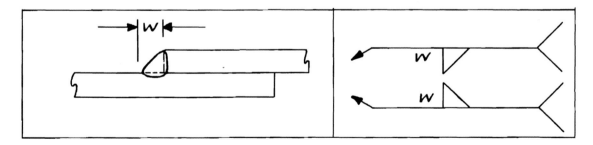

*See note on page 53.

TEE JOINTS

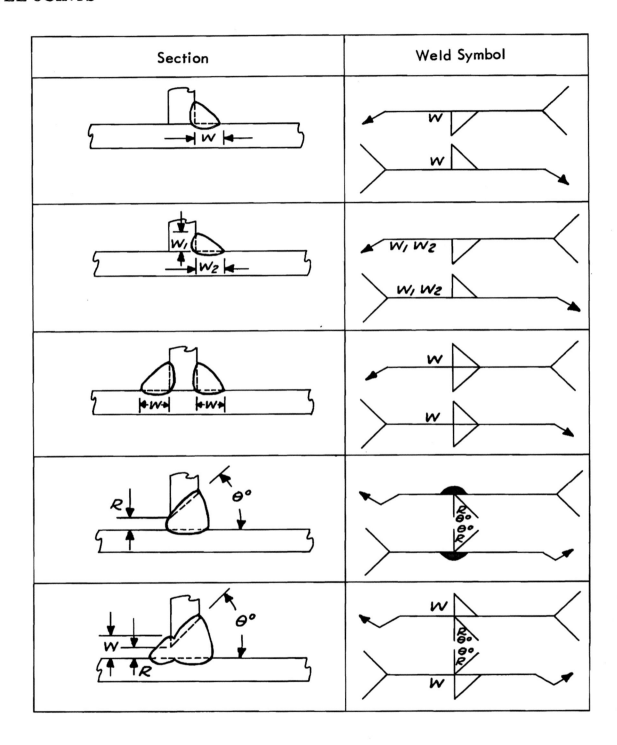

Section	Weld Symbol

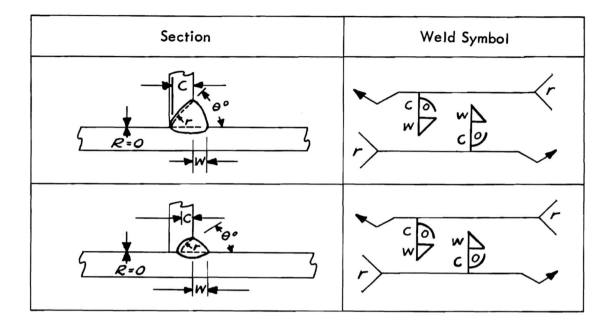

Section	Weld Symbol

The following figures have been included as further explanations of the arrow-side weld and other-side weld meanings, adequacy of symbolizing, section or end view interpretation, and the use of intermittent weld symbols. Physical dimensions are used for illustrative purposes and indicate good practice. Practical experience may find dimension differences existing.

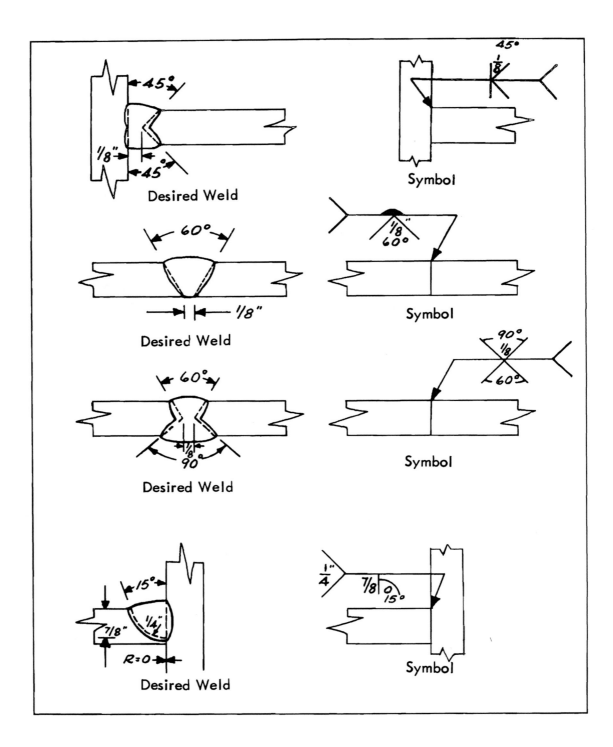

Fig. 49. Designation of Groove Angle of Groove Welds.

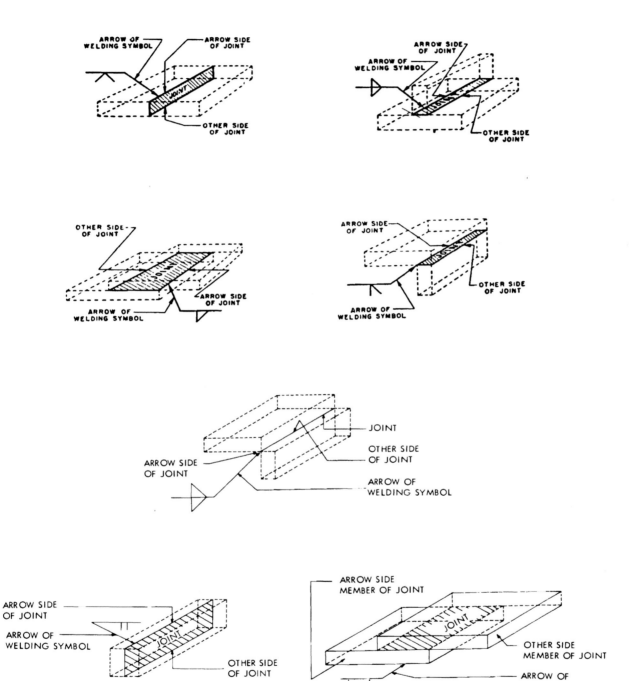

Fig. 50. Identification of Arrow Side and Other Side of Joint and "Arrow-Side" and "Other-Side" Member of Joint.

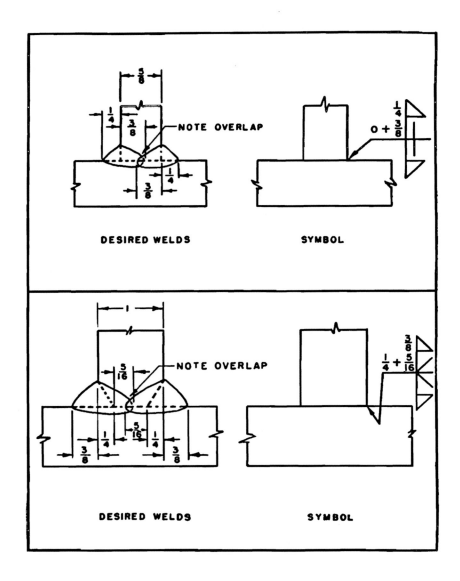

Fig. 51. Designation of Size of Combined Welds with Specified Root Penetration.

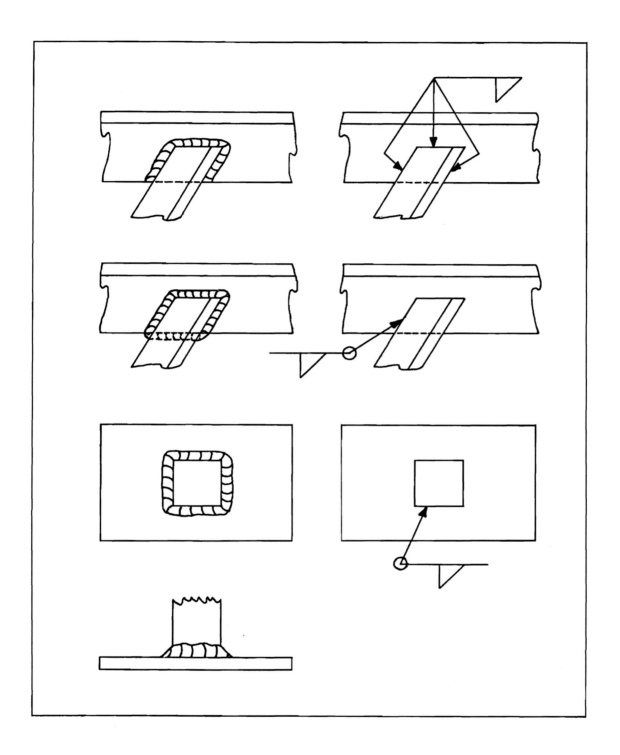

Fig. 52. Designation of Extent of Welding.

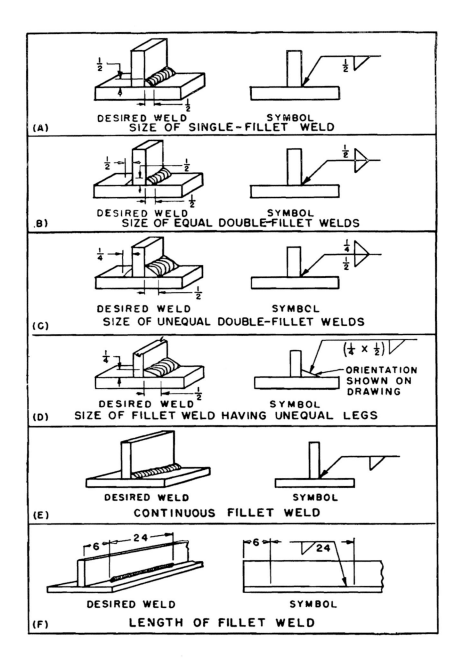

Fig. 53. Application of Dimensions to Continuous Fillet Welding Symbols.

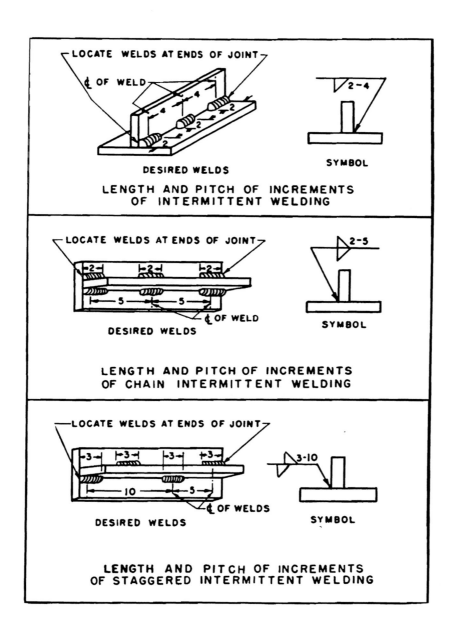

Fig. 54. Application of Dimensions to Intermittent Fillet Welding Symbols.

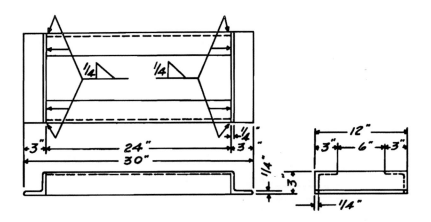

Fig. 55. Complete Shop Drawing of Welded Base.

The base used in the first drawing of this book is a simple, satisfactory example of welded construction, for it is a common type of fabrication. Figure 55 is the complete shop drawing of that base with welding symbols and dimensions shown, and the drawing made to 1/8 actual size. As the symbols indicate, the angles are to be fillet welded on the inside (the other side with respect to the arrow) with a 1/4 inch fillet weld.

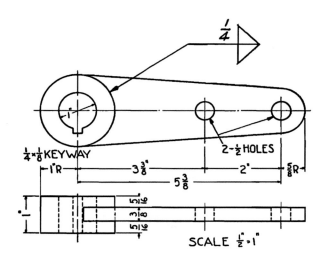

Fig. 56. Complete Shop Drawing of Lever Arm.

The lever shown in Figures 21 and 31 is very easily fabricated by welding. The cylindrical part could be cut from 2'' round stock, the hole drilled, and a keyway cut. Cutting the lever arm to shape could be done in different ways, but the final operation would be welding the two pieces together. A 1/4'' fillet weld on both sides of the arm as it meets the cylindrical piece would be sufficient, as indicated in Figure 56.

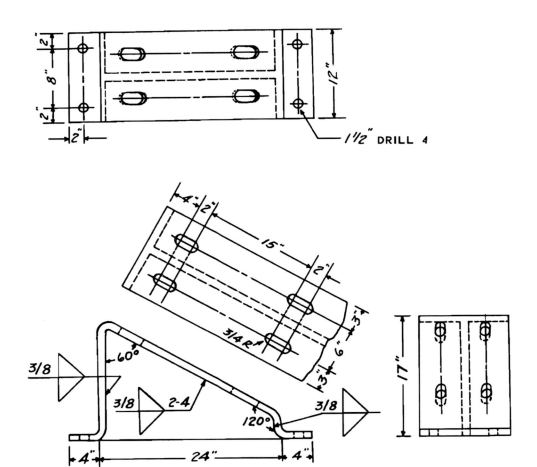

Fig. 57. Complete Shop Drawing of Slanting Base.

The slanting base of Figure 37 is another example of a welded part that is easily and cheaply fabricated from ordinary mild steel plate. The entire base consists of only two parts. One is the outline form which was bent from a piece of steel plate. The other is the central bracing plate—shown by dotted lines in the top, auxiliary and side views—which was cut from the same type of plate and welded in place. Welds are indicated in Figure 57. Notice that the symbol must be repeated at every change in direction of the line of welding. A noncontinuous weld is shown at the upper intersection. Observe how 2" long fillet welds, 4" center-to-center, both sides, are expressed. Three-eighths (3/8) inch is size of fillet welds (the length of the fillet leg).

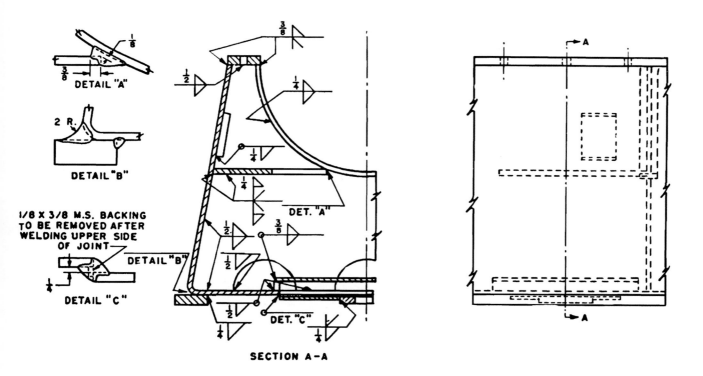

Fig. 58. Use of Arc Welding Symbols on Machinery Drawing.

Figure 58 is a reproduction of a standard instruction drawing. The subject is a large welded gear housing and is pictured in the front and section views. The welding symbols indicate both the type and size of weld at each joint. Included also are detailed welded joints, where standard symbols should be explained further to the welder to avoid any misunderstanding on the proper welding instructions. This drawing should be studied carefully to make certain that all welds are properly identified. This is a good check on your understanding of welding symbols explained earlier in this book.

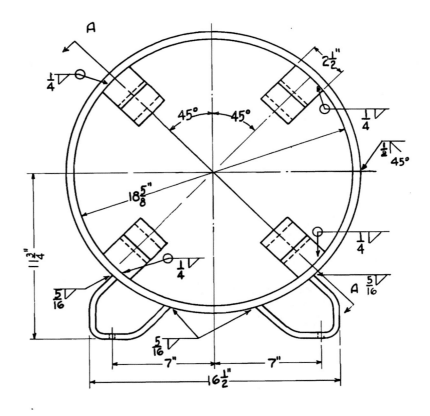

Fig. 59. Motor Frame.

Shop drawings are sometimes made especially for the welder—omitting all of the machining dimensions—but including all of the dimensions necessary for assembly and welding. As the welder quite often gets formed pieces to assemble and weld, he is not so much interested in how they are formed as he is in the assembly proportions. Figures 59 and 59-A show a motor frame to be welded together from 10 different parts. The dimensions necessary are those which will locate all of these parts in their correct relative positions. It can be seen on the drawing that in this case the centerline dimensions are very important. Since the feet and cross supports are formed when the welder gets them, they are not dimensioned but locating dimensions for assembly are given.

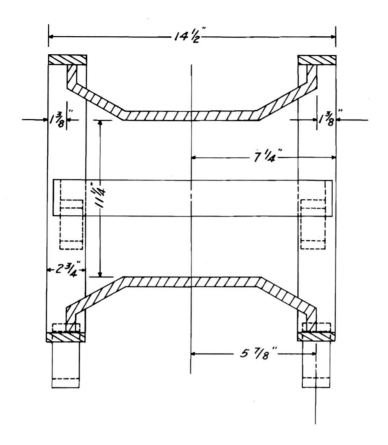

Fig. 59-A. Section A-A of Motor Frame.

The section—A-A may seem strange at first but after consideration it will be seen that this type of section cutting gives the cleanest view and supplies the needed information. Carefully study the welding symbols. How would you weld this frame?

1. According to the symbol which side (as you look at the sheet) of the butt weld on the rings is beveled? Does it make any differences in this case?

2. What is the root opening of the bevel butt weld?

3. What is the included angle of the beveling?

4. Is the bead of this bevel weld to be flush with the ring surface?

(Answers to these questions can be found on page 175.)

Another practical example of welded fabrication is shown in Figure 60. This boss is constructed of 1/4'' mild sheet steel cut and bent to the desired shape. The box-like construction is apparent from the drawing.

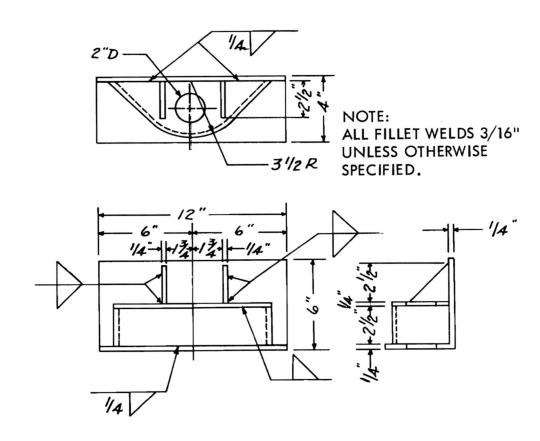

NOTE:
ALL FILLET WELDS 3/16"
UNLESS OTHERWISE
SPECIFIED.

Fig. 60.

QUESTIONS:

1. How many pieces are cut to form this boss?
2. Can all of the parts be assembled in their proper position before any welding is done?

(Answers to these questions can be found on page 175.)

PRACTICE IN READING
SHOP DRAWINGS

Study each of the drawings in this section carefully. Make sure that you understand the *meaning* of each line and each instruction. Try to visualize — to see in your mind's-eye — the finished appearance of each object and each part of it. Then, in the space below the drawing, or on the facing page, make a sketch, or pictorial drawing of the object *as you see it.*

Compare your sketches with the perspective drawing, or the photograph, shown on the next page. Then, as you check your drawing and the drawing or photograph given in the book, try to decide how you would go about making the object.

Make an effort to sketch *each one* of these objects as accurately as you can. This type of practice is the best way to develop speed and accuracy in reading shop drawings.

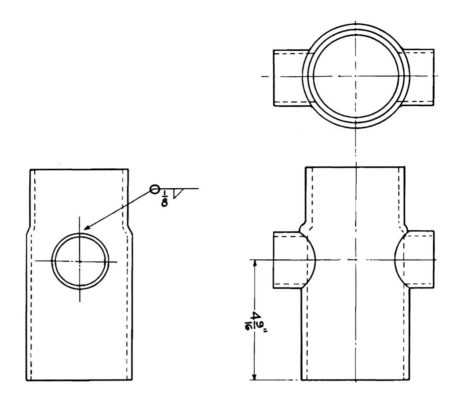

Fig. 61. Air Duct Assembly.

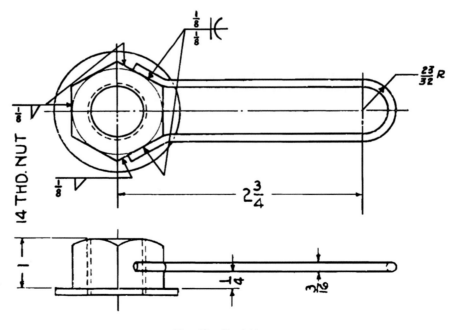

Fig. 62. Reel Nut.

HOW TO READ SHOP DRAWINGS

USE THIS PAGE FOR YOUR SKETCHES OF FIGURES 61 AND 62.

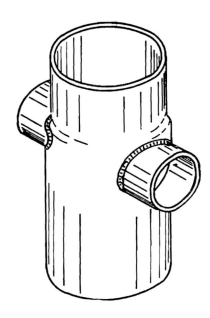

Fig. 61-A.

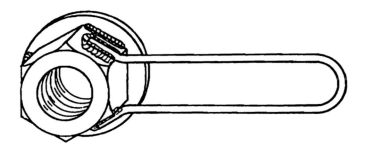

Fig. 62-A.

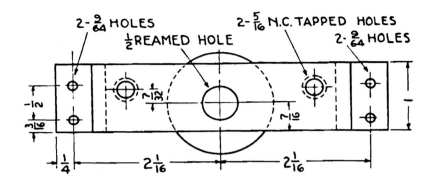

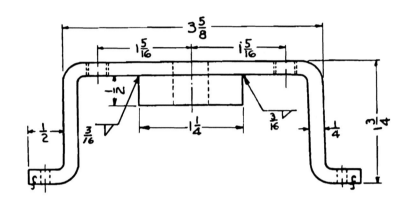

Fig. 63. Switch Bracket.

DRAW THE SWITCH BRACKET IN THIS SPACE

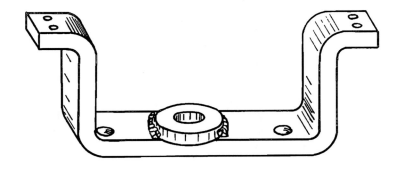

Fig. 63-A.

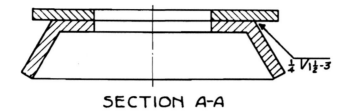

SECTION A-A

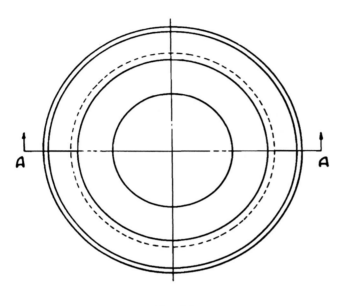

Fig. 64.

USE THIS SPACE FOR YOUR SKETCH

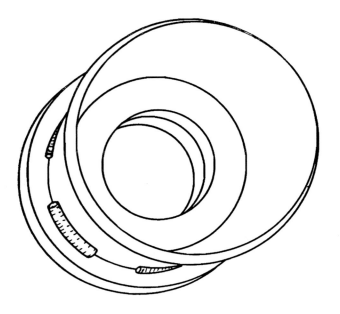

Fig. 64-A.

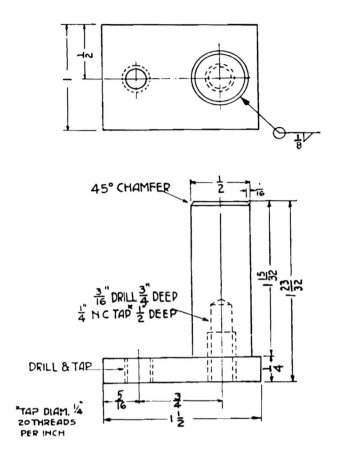

Fig. 65. Switch Arm.

DRAW THE SWITCH ARM BELOW

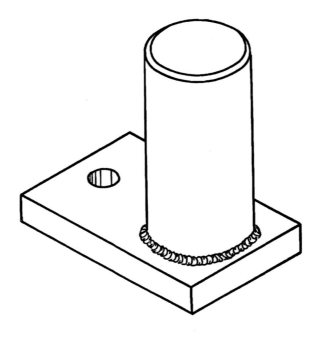

Fig. 65-A.

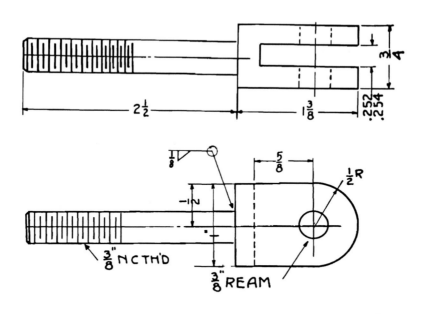

Fig. 66. Drive Link End

USE SPACE BELOW FOR YOUR SKETCH—THEN
COMPARE WITH FIG. 66-A ON PAGE 90

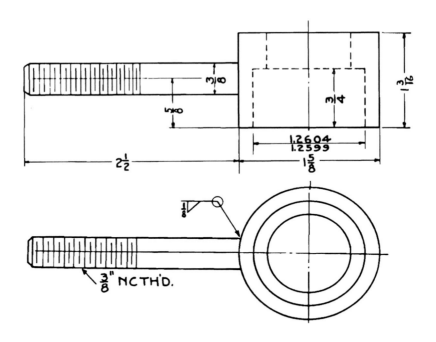

Fig. 67. Drive Collar.

SKETCH THE DRIVE COLLAR BELOW BEFORE YOU LOOK AT FIG. 67-A ON PAGE 90

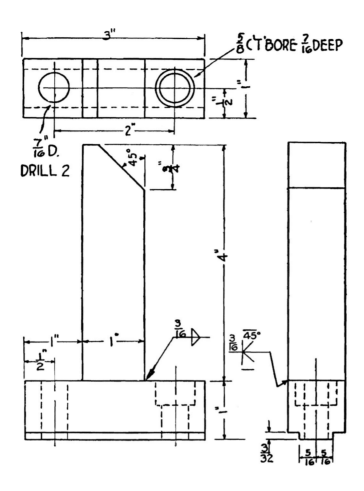

Fig. 68.

USE THE SPACE BELOW FOR YOUR SKETCH

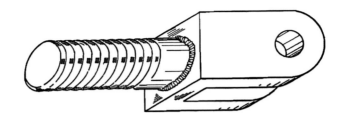

Fig. 66-A.

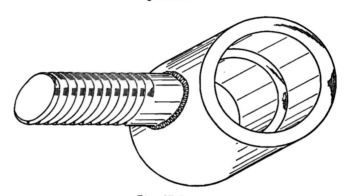

Fig. 67-A.

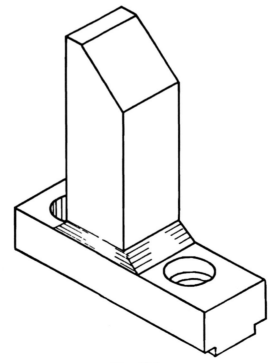

Fig. 68-A.

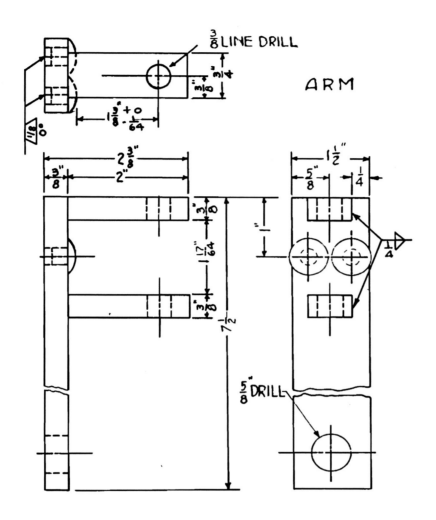

Fig. 69. Arm.

DRAW THE ARM IN THIS SPACE—THEN COMPARE WITH FIG. 69-A ON PAGE 94

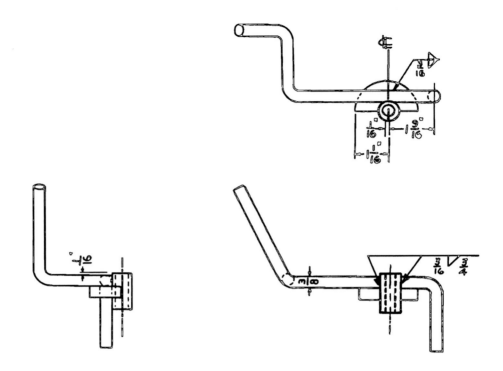

Fig. 70. Cam.

USE THIS SPACE FOR YOUR SKETCH BEFORE
CHECKING FIG. 70-A ON PAGE 94

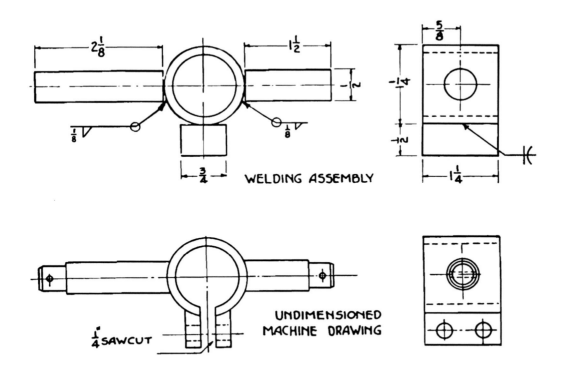

$2\frac{1}{8}$ $1\frac{1}{2}$ $\frac{1}{2}$

$\frac{1}{8}$ $\frac{1}{8}$

$\frac{3}{4}$ WELDING ASSEMBLY

$\frac{5}{8}$ $1\frac{1}{4}$ $\frac{1}{2}$ $1\frac{1}{4}$

$\frac{1}{4}''$SAWCUT   UNDIMENSIONED MACHINE DRAWING

Fig. 71. Yoke.

SKETCH THE YOKE IN THIS SPACE

93

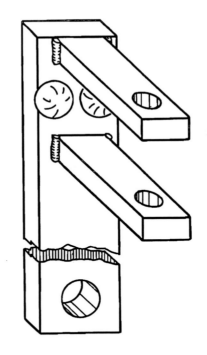

Fig. 69-A.

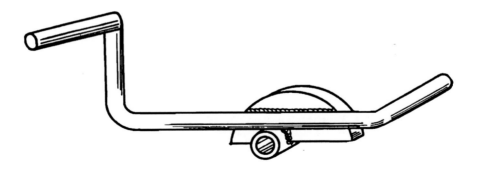

Fig. 70-A.

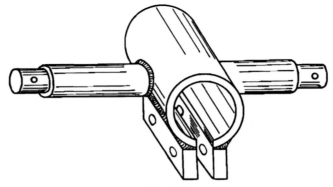

Fig. 71-A.

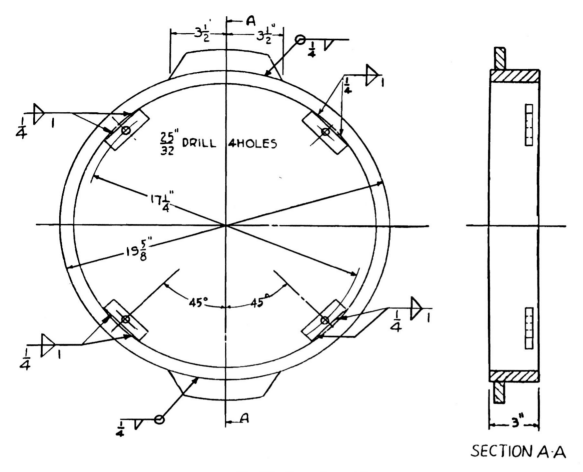

Fig. 72. Motor Frame Ring.

USE THE SPACE BELOW FOR YOUR SKETCH

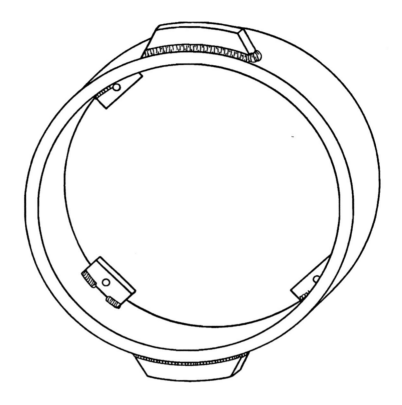

Fig. 72-A.

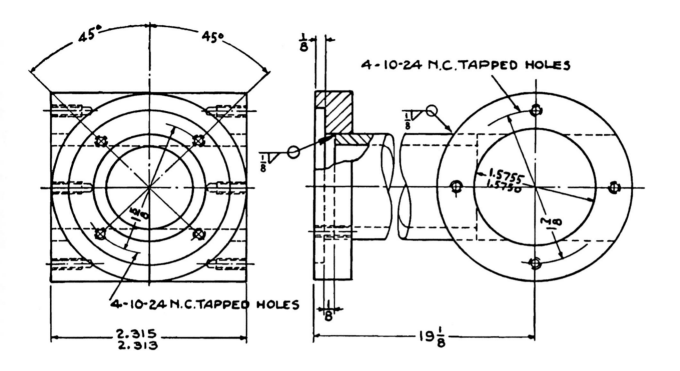

Fig. 73. Bearing Housing.

SKETCH THE BEARING HOUSING IN THIS SPACE

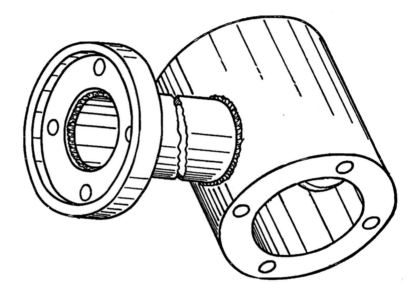

Fig. 73-A.

USE THIS SPACE
FOR YOUR SKETCHES

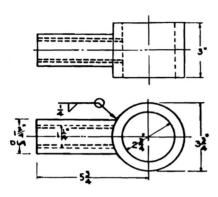

Fig. 74.

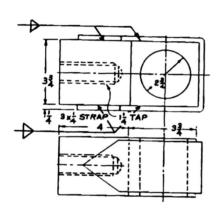

Fig. 75.

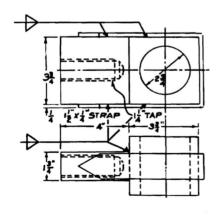

Fig. 76.

99

Fig. 74-A.

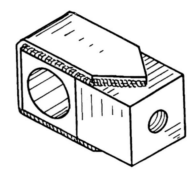

Fig. 75-A.

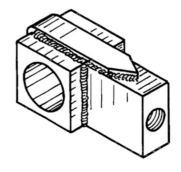

Fig. 76-A.

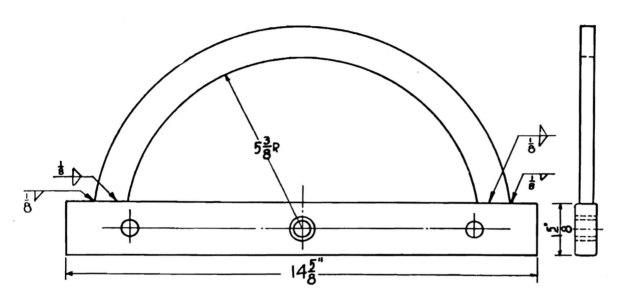

Fig. 77. Quadrant Assembly.

DRAW THE QUADRANT ASSEMBLY BELOW

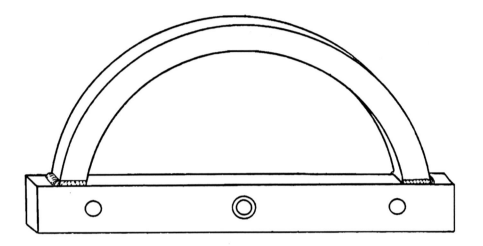

Fig. 77-A.

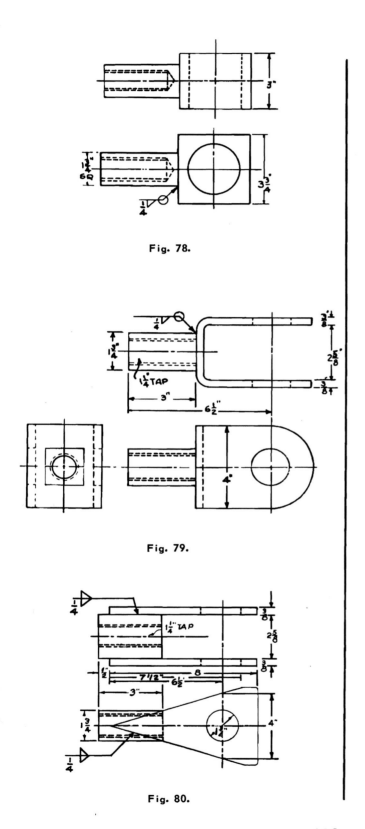

Fig. 78.

Fig. 79.

Fig. 80.

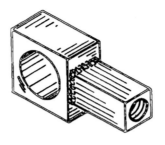

Fig. 78-A.

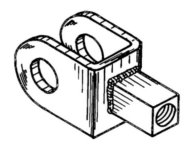

Fig. 79-A.

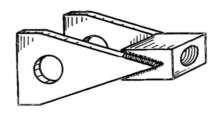

Fig. 80-A.

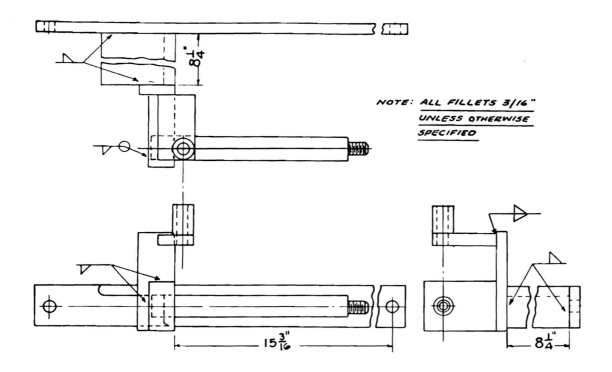

NOTE: ALL FILLETS 3/16"
UNLESS OTHERWISE
SPECIFIED

Fig. 81. Reel Bracket.

DRAW THE REEL BRACKET BELOW

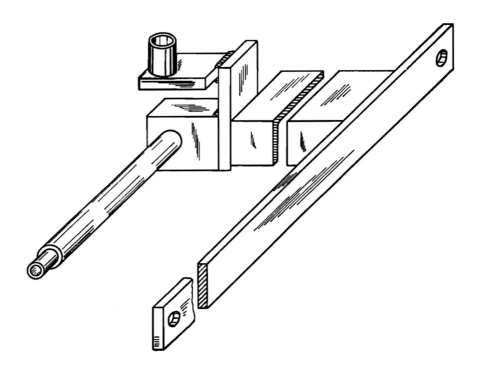

Fig. 81-A.

ACKNOWLEDGEMENT

The following examples of welded machinery have been made possible through the cooperation of The Wellman Engineering Company, Cleveland, Ohio; The Euclid Road Machinery Company, Euclid, Ohio and The Cleveland Trencher Company, Euclid, Ohio. Actual working drawings shown on right hand pages are illustrated with corresponding photographs on succeeding left hand pages to help identify each design detail.

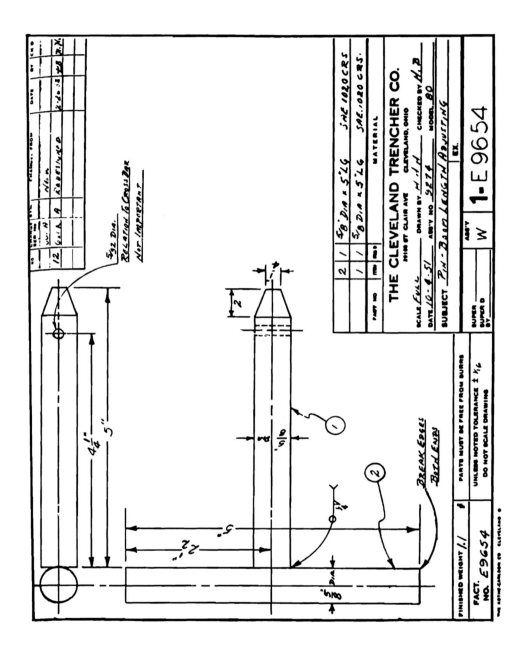

Fig. 82.

Fig. 82-A.

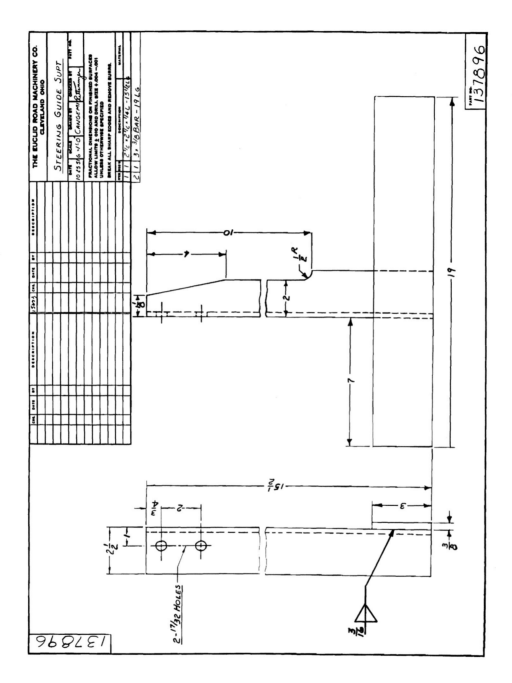

Fig. 83.

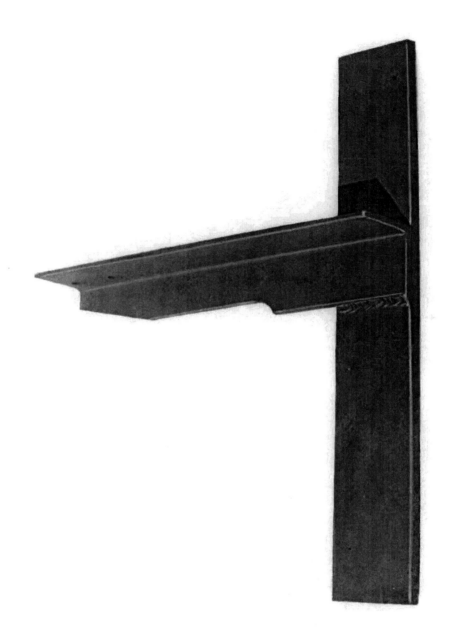

Fig. 83-A.

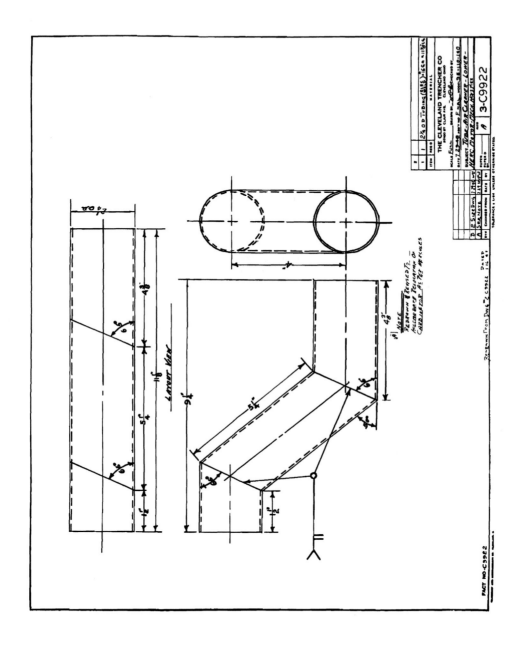

Fig. 84.

111

Fig. 84-A.

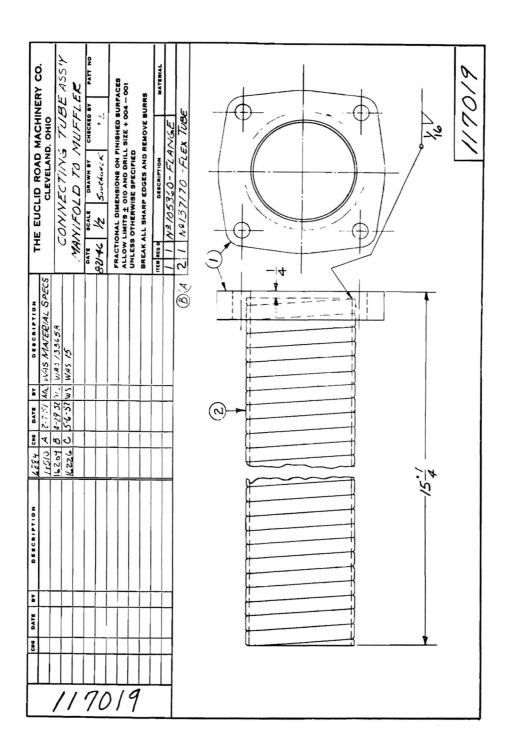

Fig. 85.

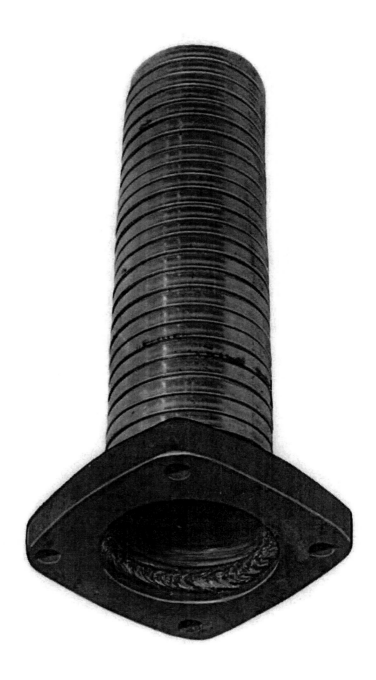

Fig. 85-A.

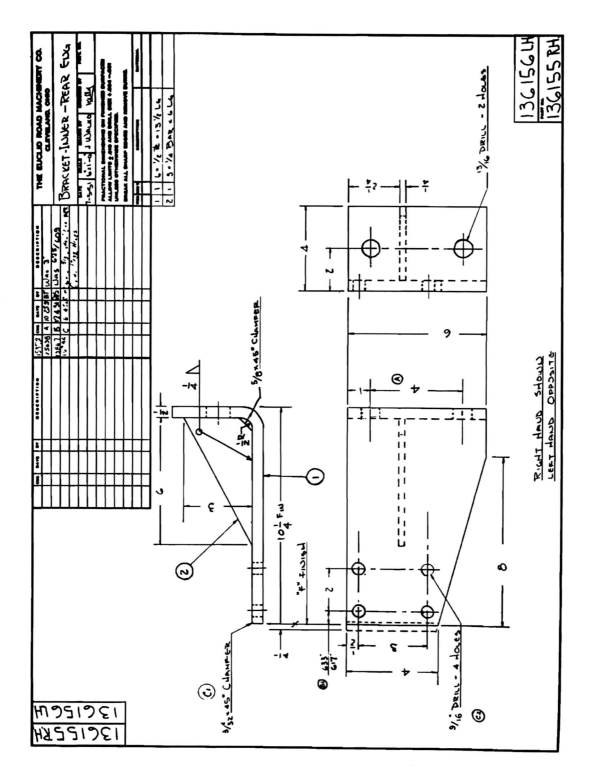

Fig. 86.

Fig. 86-A.

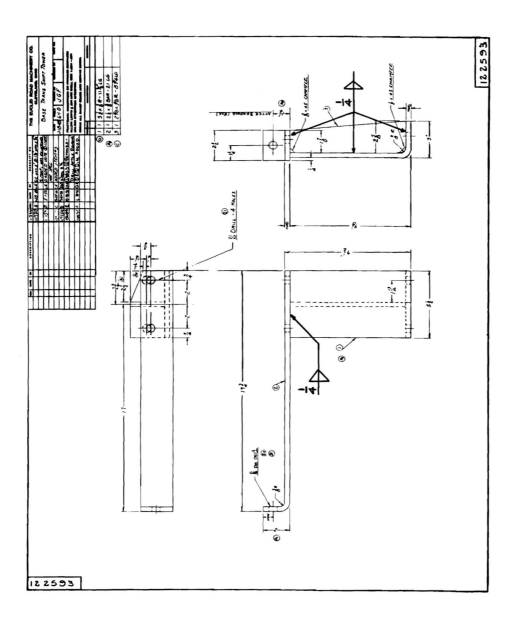

Fig. 87.

Fig. 87-A.

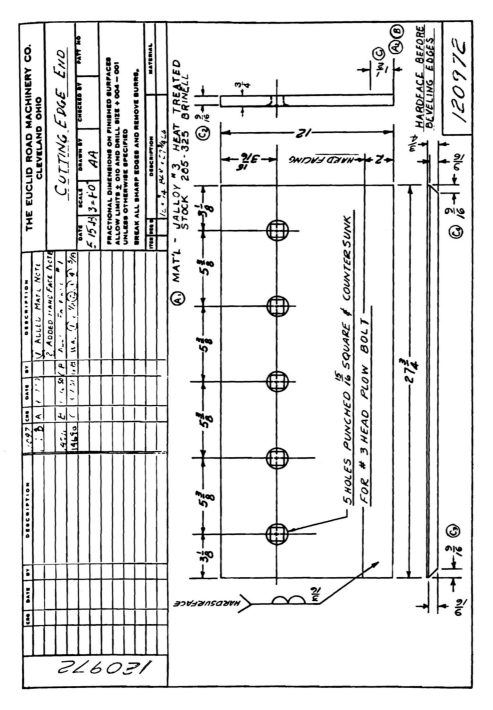

Fig. 88.

Fig. 88-A.

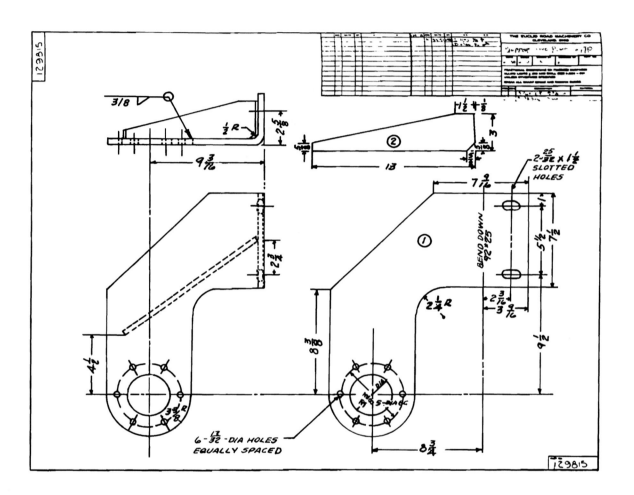

Fig. 89.

121

Fig. 89-A.

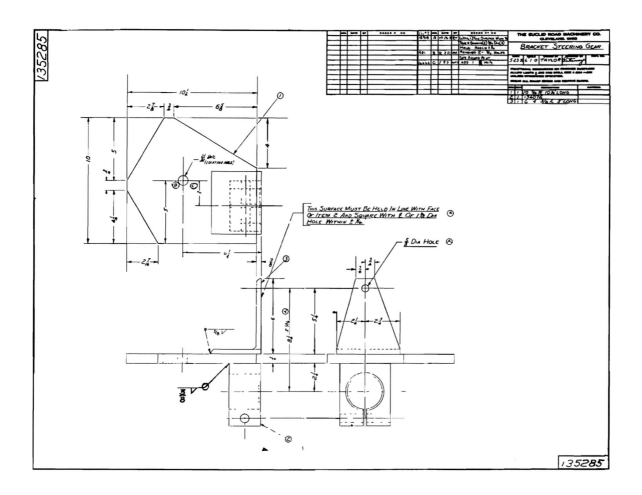

Fig. 90.

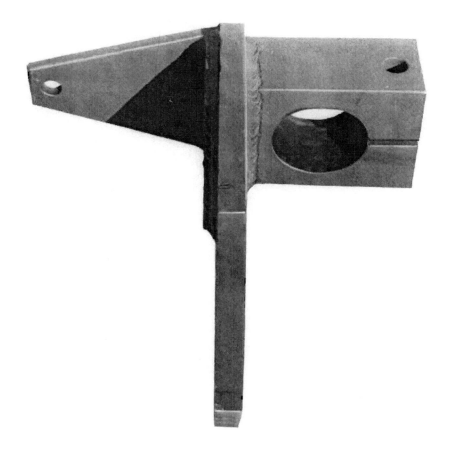

Fig. 90-A.

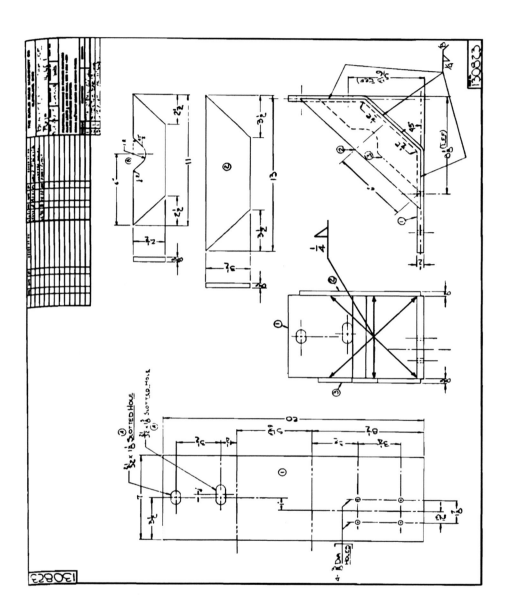

Fig. 91.

Fig. 91-A.

HOW TO READ SHOP DRAWINGS

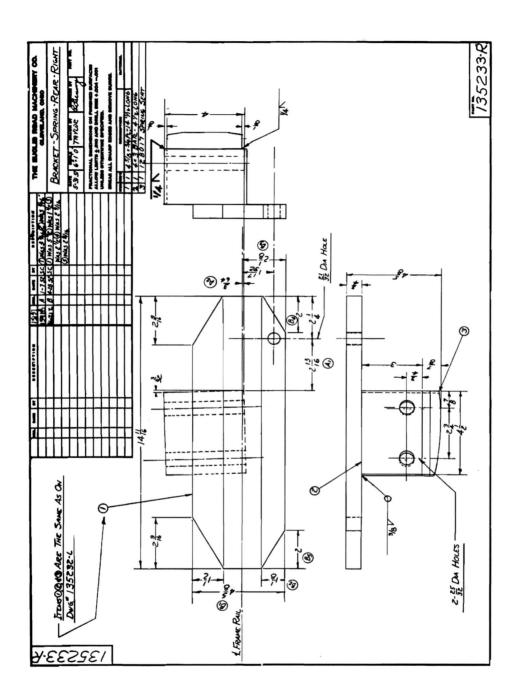

Fig. 92.

127

Fig. 92-A.

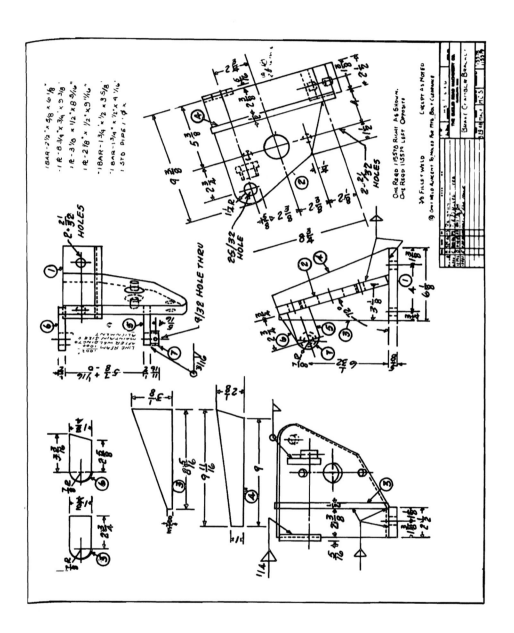

Fig. 93.

Fig. 93-A.

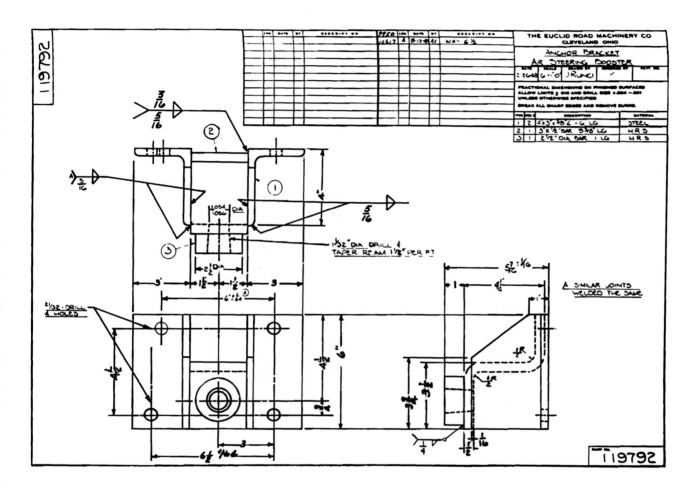

Fig. 94.

131

Fig. 94-A.

HOW TO READ SHOP DRAWINGS

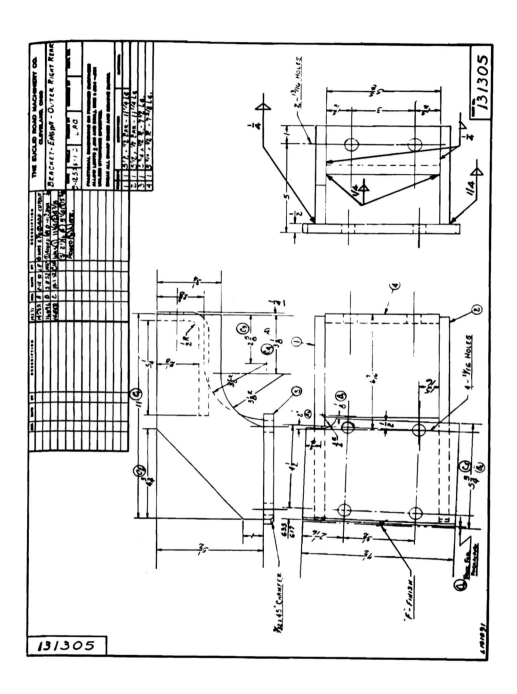

Fig. 95.

133

Fig. 95-A.

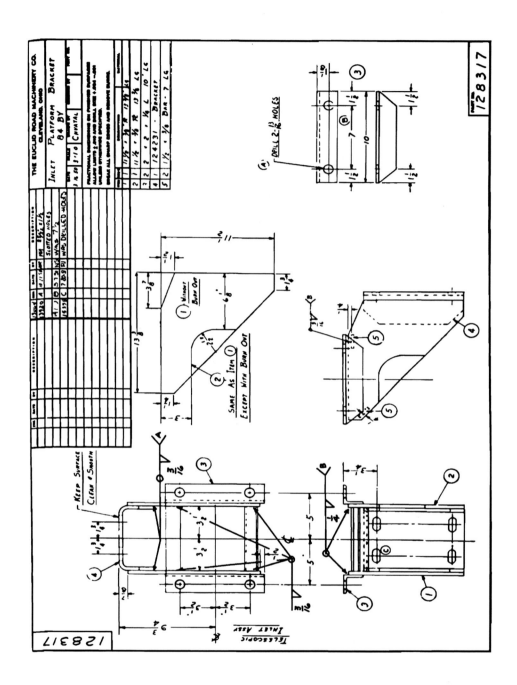

Fig. 96.

Fig. 96-A.

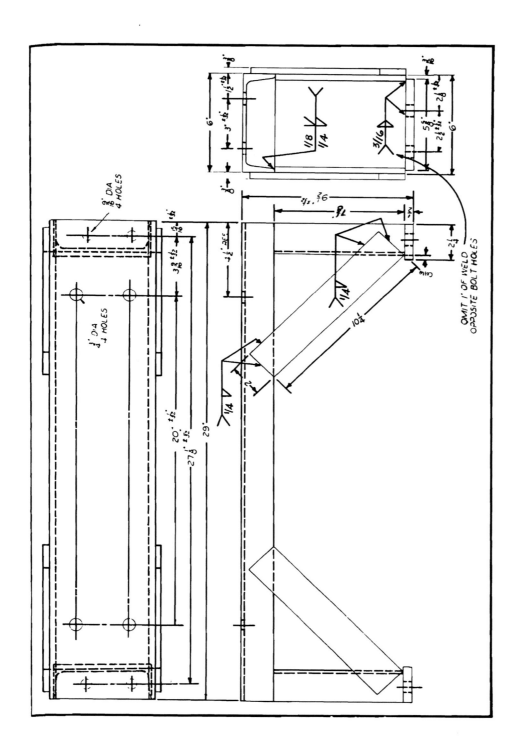

Fig. 97.

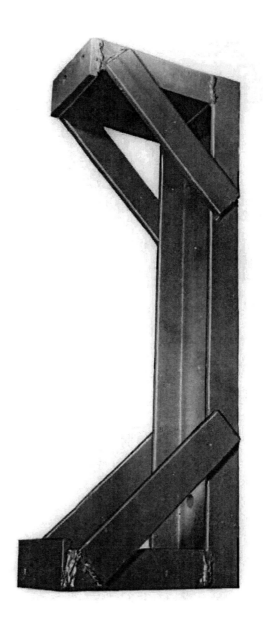

Fig. 97-A.

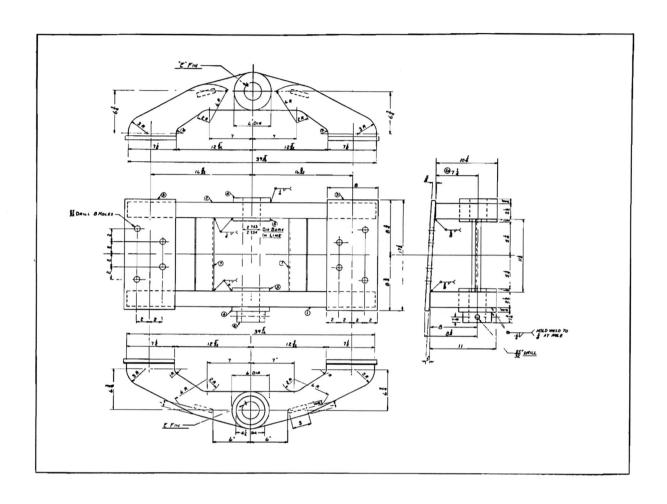

Fig. 98.

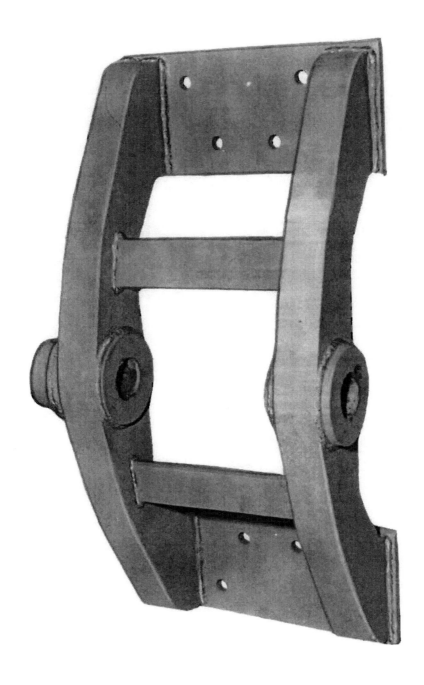

Fig. 98-A.

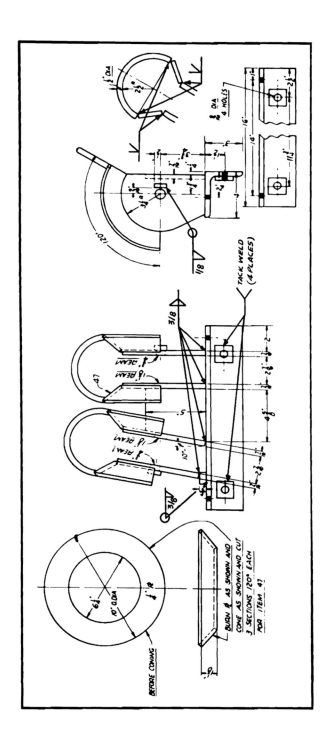

Fig. 99.

Fig. 99-A.

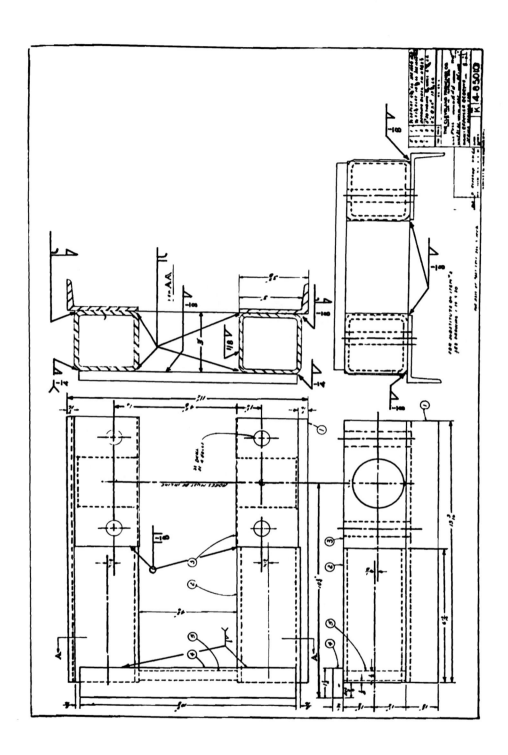

Fig. 100.

Fig. 100-A.

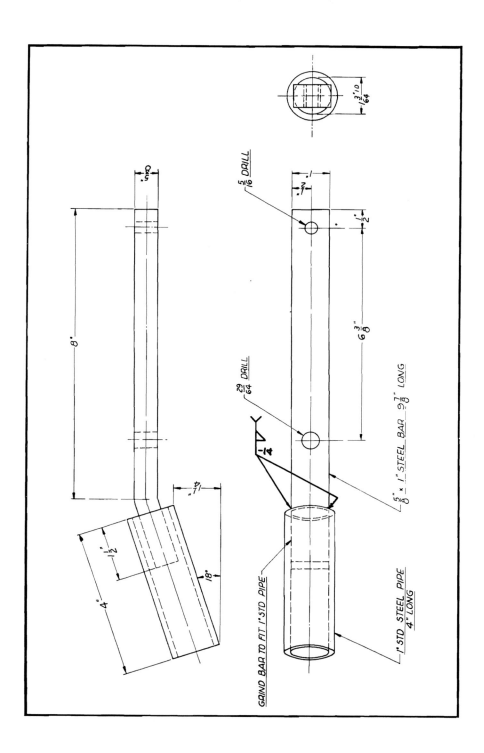

Fig. 101.

Fig. 101-A.

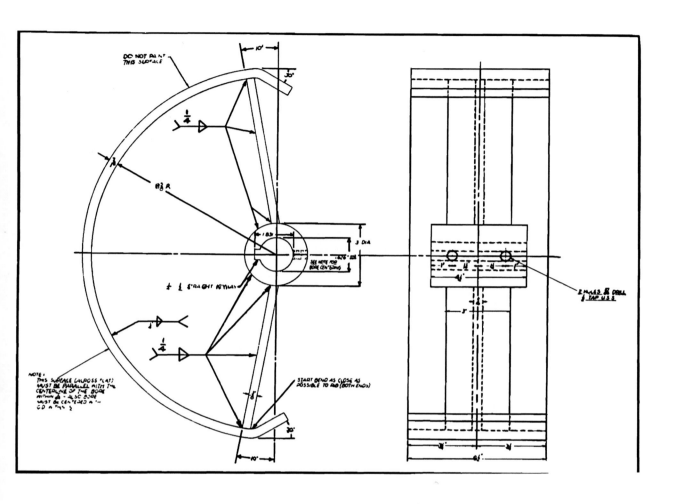

Fig. 102.

Fig. 102-A.

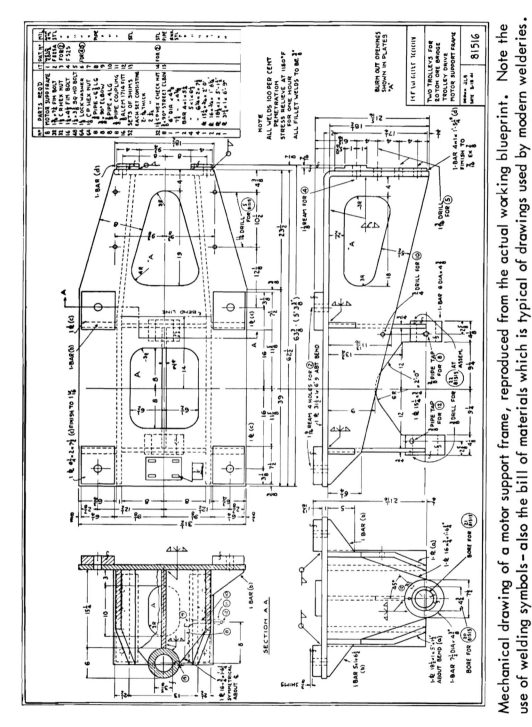

Fig. 103.

Mechanical drawing of a motor support frame, reproduced from the actual working blueprint. Note the use of welding symbols—also the bill of materials which is typical of drawings used by modern welderies.

Courtesy of Wellman Engineering Co., Cleveland, Ohio.

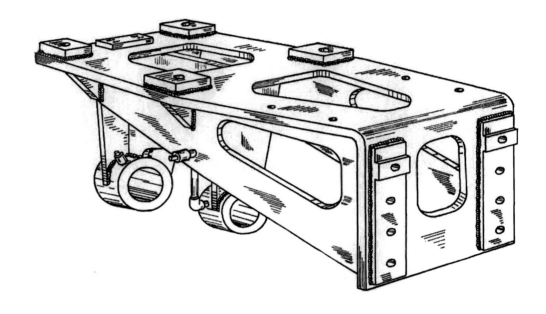

Fig. 103-A.

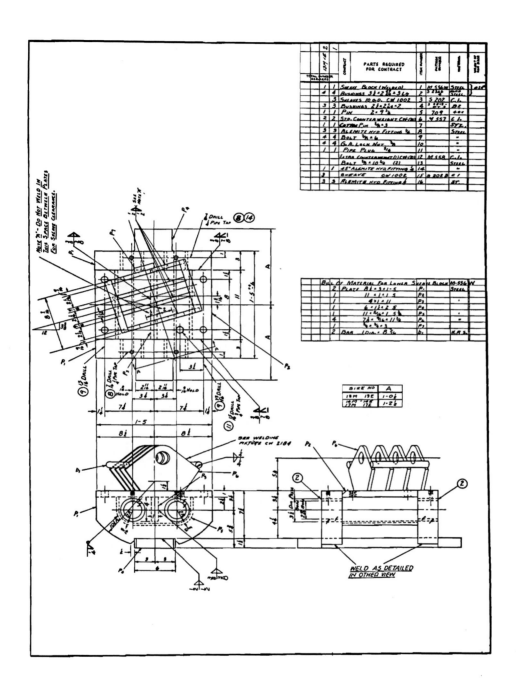

Fig. 104.

151

Fig. 104-A.

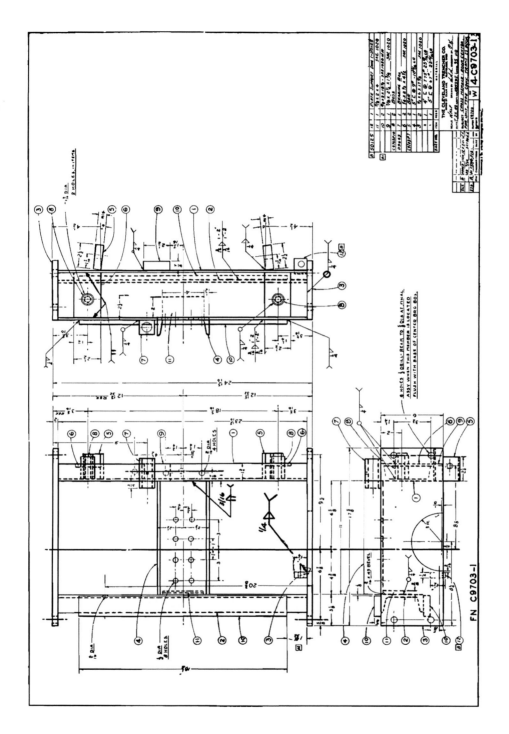

Fig. 105.

153

Fig. 105-A.

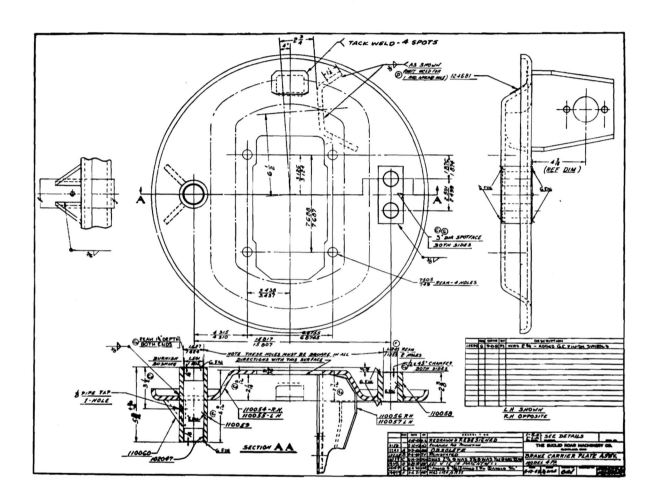

Fig. 106.

Fig. 106-A.

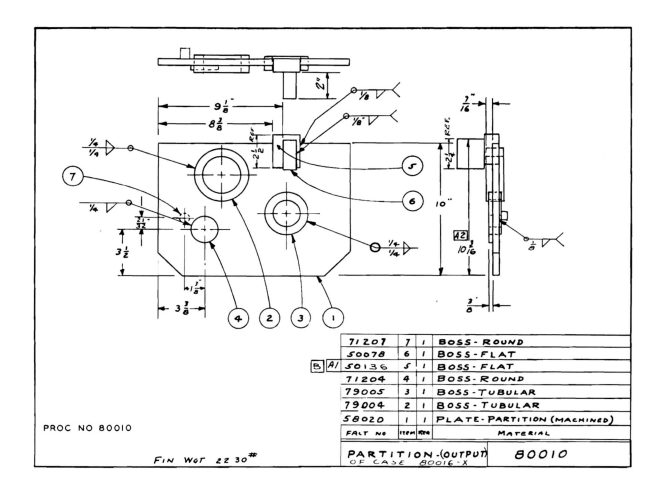

PROC NO 80010

FIN WGT 2230[#]

71207	7	I	BOSS - ROUND
50078	6	I	BOSS - FLAT
50136	5	I	BOSS - FLAT
71204	4	I	BOSS - ROUND
79005	3	I	BOSS - TUBULAR
79004	2	I	BOSS - TUBULAR
58020	I	I	PLATE - PARTITION (MACHINED)
FALT NO	ITEM	REQ	MATERIAL
PARTITION - (OUTPUT OF CASE 80016-X			80010

Fig. 107.

Fig. 107-A.

OTHER TYPES OF DRAWINGS

The examples previously shown in this workbook have been of machine or shop type drawings. Other types of drawings should also be studied. The fundamentals are the same but details may be peculiar to certain fields.

STRUCTURAL DRAWINGS

Structural drawings such as those shown in figures 108 through 110 are another application of the basic ideas discussed in the first part of this book. The reader who is interested in this field should procure a good structural handbook and acquaint himself with the variety of materials used in this field and the accepted method of representing these materials in drawings.

For any particular job, a structural drawing consists of a group of drawings. The sheets of drawings in this group can be classified as follows:

1. General Plan — May include a profile of the ground-location of structure —clearances—water levels, etc.

2. Stress Diagram — Containing main dimensions—loading stresses separately and total—size of members—typical sections of all built members showing arrangement of material, etc.

3. Shop Drawings — Shop detail drawings for all steel and iron work and all information necessary for fabricating the various parts of the structure, such as welding specifications.

4. Foundation or Masonry Plan — Detail drawings of all walls; piers; foundations quality of masonry and mortar, etc.

5. Erection Diagram — Showing relative location of every part of the structure. All main dimensions—shipping marks, etc.

6. Falsework Plans — If the falsework for masonry—concrete, etc., is designed in the office the drawings are included.

7. Bills of Material.

8. List of Drawings.

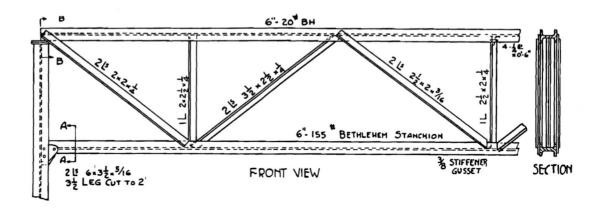

FRONT VIEW

SECTION

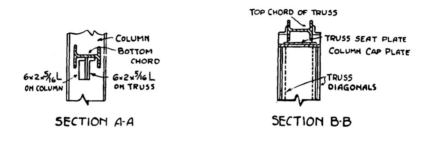

SECTION A-A   SECTION B-B

Fig. 108.

In Figure 108 a front (elevation) view is shown (with a number of section views clarifying the details) of an arc welded building truss.

Note the use of dimensions such as

2 ∟s   2½x2x3/16   What does this mean?*

*The member is made up of two standard "angle iron" pieces, the angle dimensions being 2-1/2" x 2" x 3/16".

The following drawings have been taken from the "Procedure Handbook of Arc Welding Design and Practice" as examples of standard welding practice. Further reading of that handbook will be very helpful in becoming acquainted with the use of welding in structural design.

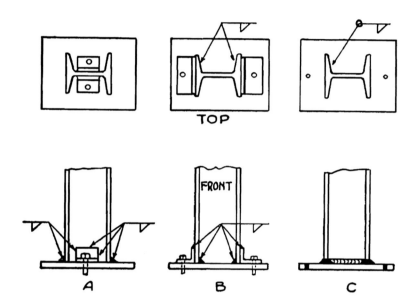

Fig. 109. Typical Details of Arc Welded Column Bases.

Study the structures in Figure 110. These examples are intended as a guide to those interested in this field.

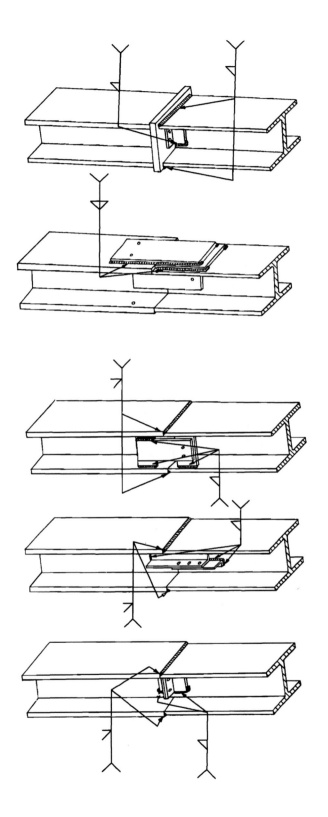

Fig. 110. Butt connection of Structural Members.

TANK DRAWINGS

Tank design and erection is a specialty which requires another application of drawing principles. Since most tanks are designed and erected to comply with existing codes, it is important that the correct procedure be set down on shop drawings.

The familiar "general plan" of tank erection will be the same as many structural drawings, but the detailed joint sections are laid out to comply with the governing code. The joints must be made as the section indicates.

The examples on the following pages illustrate the standard procedure for indicating and welding various joints.

Some of the material in the following few pages was furnished through the courtesy of The Chicago Bridge and Iron Works.

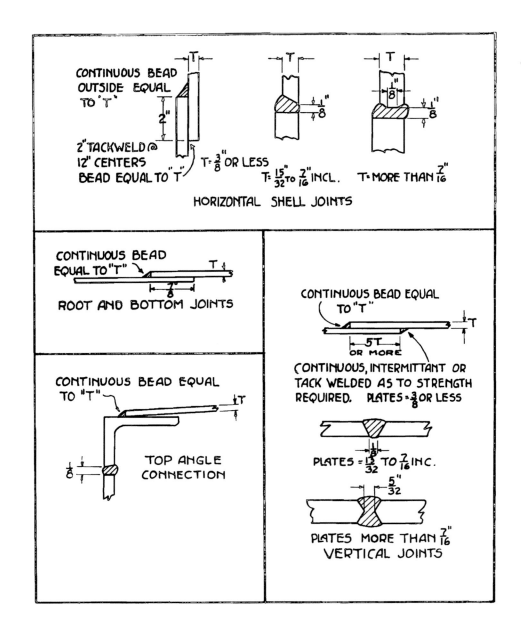

Fig. 111. Standard Welding Details for All Welded Storage Tanks with Butt Welded and Lap Welded Shells. (Sheet 1)

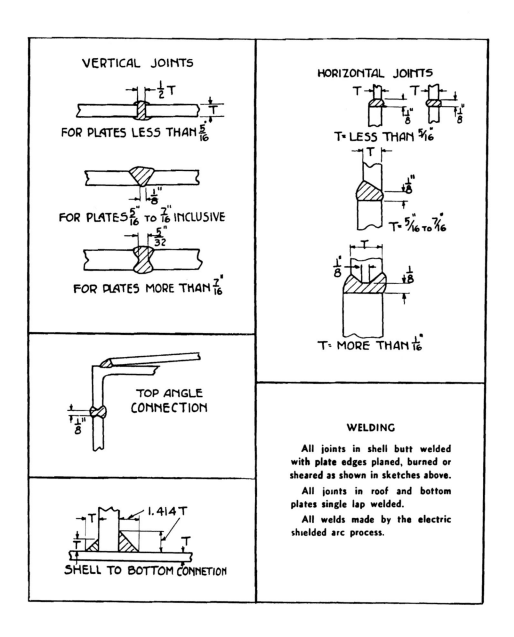

Fig. 111. Standard Welding Details for all Welded Storage Tanks with Butt Welded and Lap Welded Shells. (Sheet 2)

PIPE DRAWINGS

Pipe drawings use a single heavy line to represent the runs of pipe. The principles of orthographic projection are followed in most cases, but isometric or oblique drawings are sometimes used—either alone or supplementary to the orthographic drawing. Valves and fittings are shown by means of symbols. Welded pipe connections, of course, are indicated by the A.W.S. symbols. Since there are many important details of construction* which must be outlined to the pipe fitter, it is essential that piping drawings contain very complete notes.

The list of symbols below was used in making the following pipe drawings. For more complete coverage, consult Engineering Drawing by French or a pipefitter's or engineer's handbook.

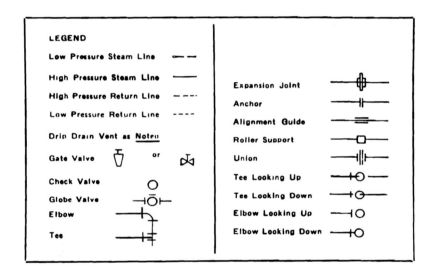

The fundamentals of the subject have been covered previously.

Study the method of presentation as it is shown here and apply the principles outlined before.

Note the simplicity of this type of drawing.

*Valve clearance for openings, pipe sizes, connection data, etc.

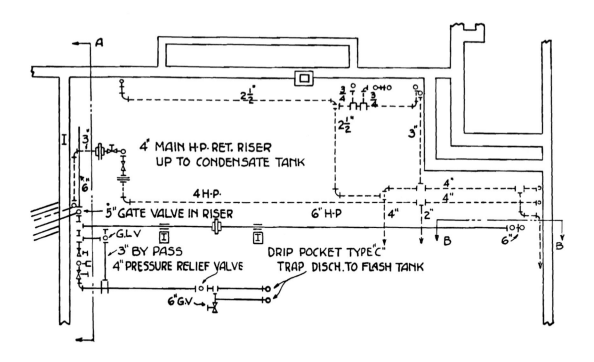

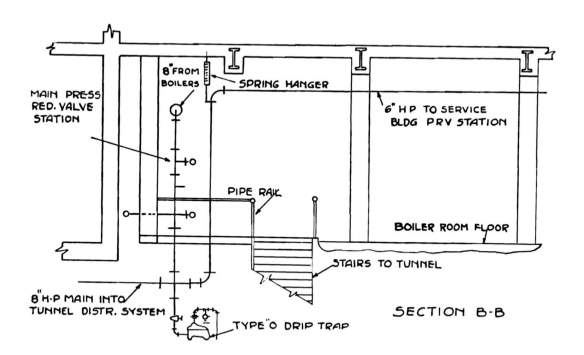

Fig. 112.

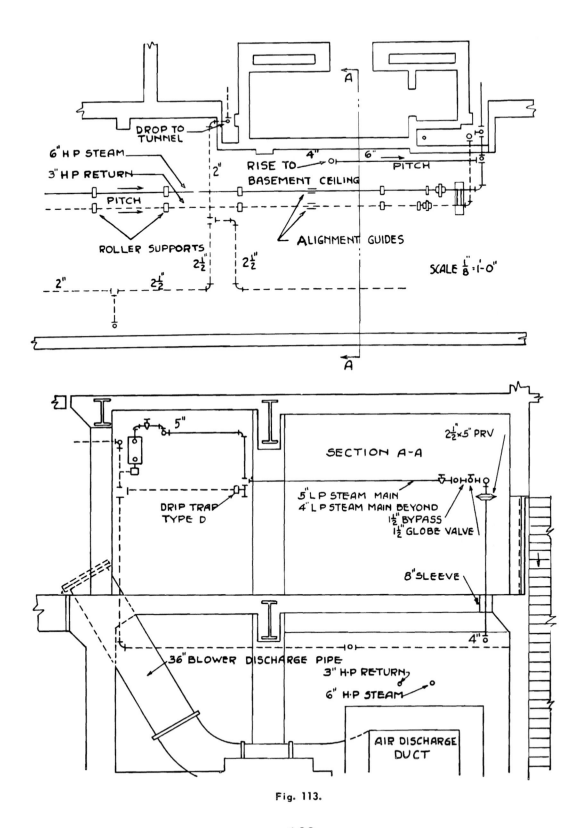

Fig. 113.

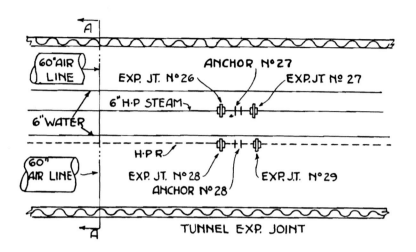

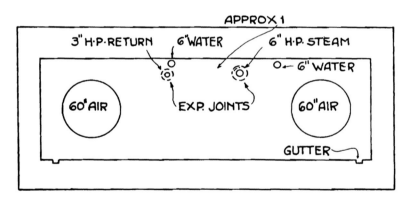

TYPICAL SECTION A-A

Fig. 114.

Practice and study are the best ways to acquire speed and accuracy in reading shop drawings after the principles are learned.

Reference to this or to any of the many good books on the subject will refresh your memory when necessary. Remember that this subject is a basis for your future education and advancement.

Intelligent and ambitious men realize that education and knowledge are essential to security and advancement in their work. Knowledge may be gained by experience or by study. Self improvement is a most rapid and enjoyable means of gaining knowledge.

Experience is necessary. The combination of experience and reading for self-improvement is the best answer to the problem of how to get ahead. For additional information on text books concerning arc welding consult the book review section in the back of this book or write directly to The Lincoln Electric Co., Cleveland 17, Ohio.

HOW TO READ SHOP DRAWINGS

QUESTIONS

Test your knowledge of drawing practices with the following questions.

Group A

1. Why should a welding operator know how to read blueprints?

2. Is a picture drawing practical for conveying fabricating information?

3. What are the types of picture drawings?

4. Of what value are picture drawings to the designer?

5. What lines are made to scale on the isometric drawing?

6. What three views form the basis for the orthographic drawing?

Group B

1. For what is the "dotted" line used?

2. For what is the "dash-dot" line used?

3. What is used to indicate the end of a dimension line?

4. On what lines do the dimension line arrow heads terminate?

5. In what kind of views are "break" lines used? How are break lines usually made.

6. Name the alphabet of lines and sketch an example of each.

Group C

1. Can complete information ever be given in less than three views?

2. Do we ever use more than 3 views in a drawing?

3. What views could be shown without deviating from the illustrated orthographic idea?

Group D

1. Why are dimension lines and figures put on drawings?

2. Are the inch marks and feet marks always put on a drawing?

3. How are dimensions placed for reading?

4. How are limits of variation or tolerances indicated on a dimension?

5. Are drawings always made full size?

6. How is the scale indicated?

Group E

1. What kind of surfaces require "auxiliary" views to give complete information?

2. From what angle do we observe a surface of this type to get the "auxiliary" view?

3. Is it necessary to have a complete view of the whole object when reading an auxiliary view?

4. Why are "sections" used?

5. How are screw threads identified? Where are the thread specifications given?

Group F

1. What information about welds does the American Welding Society symbol give?

2. Is the arrow used for each symbol?

3. If only one member of a grooved weld is to be grooved how do we know which one it is?

4. List all of the types of arc welds and give the basic symbol for each.

5. Is a grooved weld always grooved the full thickness of the member?

6. Is the depth of grooving specified on the symbol? Where?

HOW TO READ SHOP DRAWINGS

ANSWERS

Group A

1. He will know exactly what is to be made and he will have a record or instruction sheet to which he can refer as the job progresses without asking his supervisor time-wasting questions.

2. No.

3. Perspective - isometric - oblique - cabinet.

4. Aids for studying appearance.

5. Vertical lines and lines at 30° to the horizontal.

6. Front, top, right side.

Group B.

1. Hidden outline.

2. Centerlines of pieces and the center of circular holes and bosses or the center of any portion of a circle arc.

3. The arrow head.

4. Extension lines. Hidden and visible outline, centerlines.

5. Views of a piece of long but unchanging section, to shorten the view and make it possible to use a smaller sheet. To eliminate unnecessary detail. Refer to pages 36 and 38.

6. Refer to the alphabet of lines, page 14.

Group C

1. Yes. For example, Figure 12 could be completely pictured with top and front views.

2. Yes. Figures 27 and 35, for example.

3. Front, top, right side, left side, bottom, and rear views.

Group D

1. To show accurately the necessary dimensional information. Although the drawing is made to scale it cannot possibly be made or remain accurate enough for measurements of this kind.

2. No. Inch marks may be omitted if all dimensions are in inches.

3. To be read from the bottom and righthand edge of the plate.

4. $10,000 \begin{smallmatrix} +.002 \\ -.000 \end{smallmatrix}$ $5 \begin{smallmatrix} +.005 \\ -.005 \end{smallmatrix}$ etc.

5. No. Refer to discussion of Scale drawings, page 28.

6. By a note - for example

    Scale 1/2" = 1"   Scale 1/8" = 1'

Group E

1. Surfaces at odd angles. Slanting or oblique surfaces.

2. At right angles to the oblique or slanting surface.

3. No. Just the surface in question is necessary.

4. To reduce the number of hidden and visible outline lines and give clearer, more easily read information about the object. To bring out certain features of shape and relationship.

5. By a standard symbol or pictorial drawing. Specifications are given in an attached note.

Group F.

1. Refer to weld symbol, page 43.

2. Yes.

3. The arrow points to it.

Group F (continued)

4.			TYPE OF WELD					
BACK OR BACKING	FILLET	PLUG OR SLOT	GROOVE				
			SQUARE	V	BEVEL	U	J
⌒	◣	▭	‖	V	⊬	Y	⊬

TYPE OF WELD					
GROOVE		FLANGE		MELT THRU	SURFACING
FLARE BEVEL	FLARE V	EDGE	CORNER		
)(	)(	JL	IL	⬤	⌣⌣

WELD ALL AROUND	FIELD WELD	CONTOUR	
		FLUSH	CONVEX
◯	●	—	⌒

5. No. Refer to groove weld illustrations, page 64.

6. Yes, left of the type symbol: Example U weld grooved 7/8" deep. See Symbol bottom Figure 49, Page 64.

Answers to questions on page 75.

1. Arrow-Lower, ... No.

2. No Root Opening.

3. 45°

4. No.

Answers to questions on page 76.

1. Five.

2. No.

GLOSSARY OF DESCRIPTIVE TERMS USED IN THE WELDING INDUSTRY

Courtesy of The American Welding Society

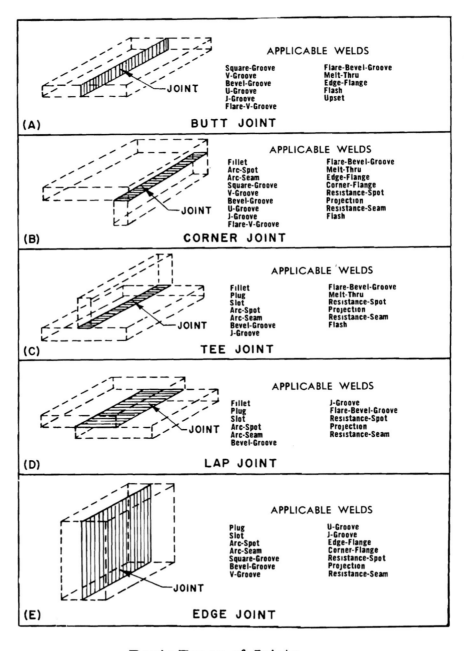

Basic Types of Joints

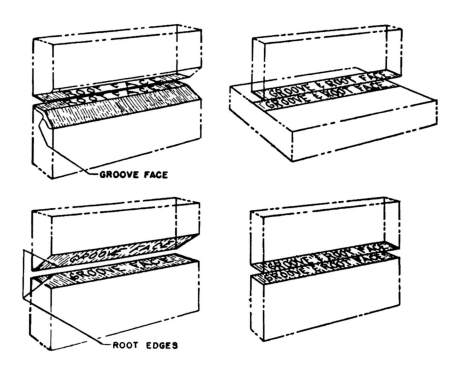

Groove Face, Root Face and Root Edge

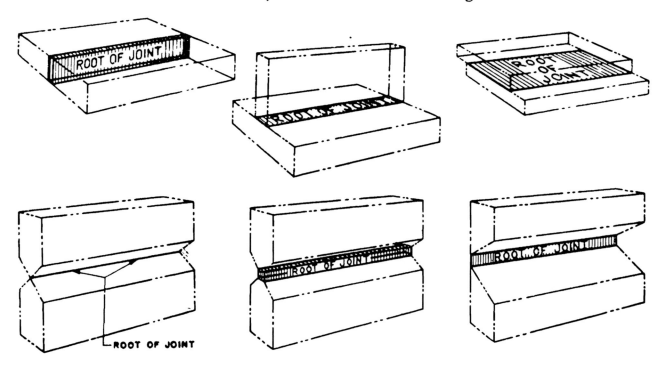

Root of Joint

177

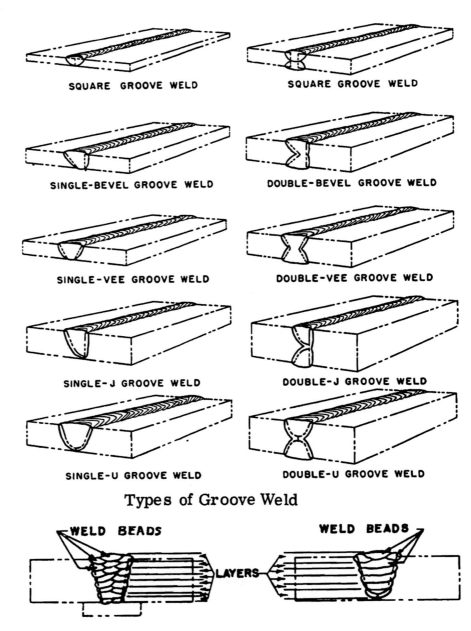

Types of Groove Weld

Weld Beads and Layers

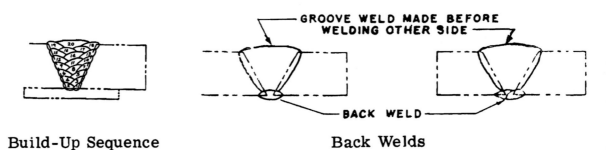

Build-Up Sequence   Back Welds

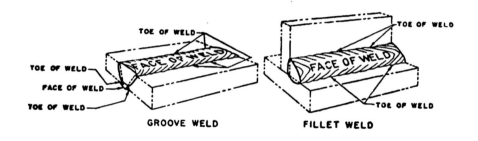

Face and Toe of Weld

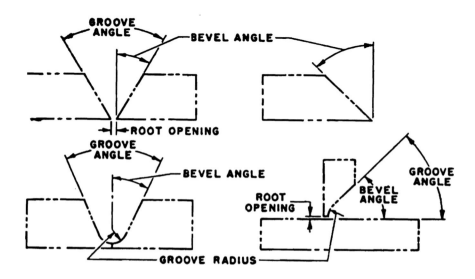

Bevel Angle, Groove Angle, Groove Radius and Root Opening

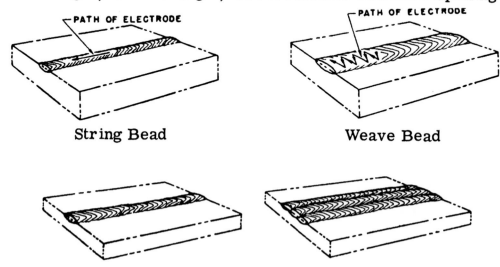

String Bead   Weave Bead

Bead Welds

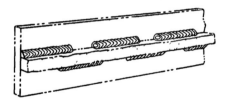

Staggered Intermittent
Fillet Welding

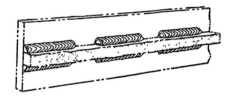

Chain Intermittent Fillet
Welding

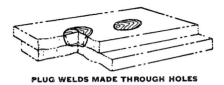

PLUG WELDS MADE THROUGH HOLES

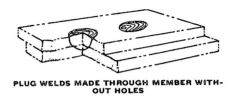

PLUG WELDS MADE THROUGH MEMBER WITH-
OUT HOLES

Plug Welds

Slot Welds

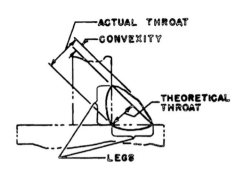

Convex Fillet Weld

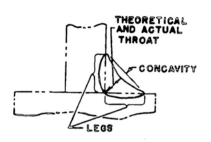

Concave Fillet Weld

180

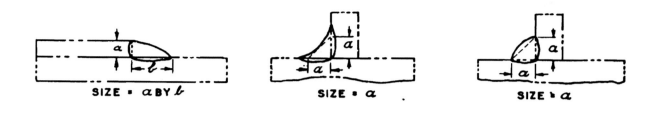

Size of Fillet Welds

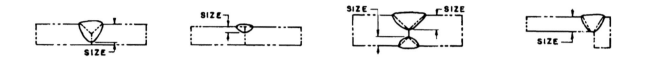

Size of Groove Welds

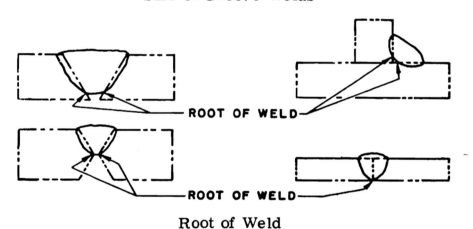

Root of Weld

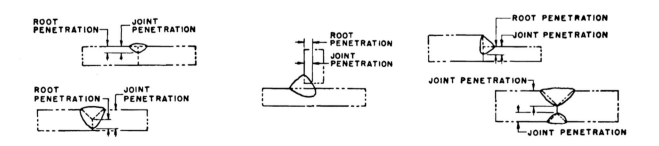

Root Penetration and Joint Penetration of Groove Welds

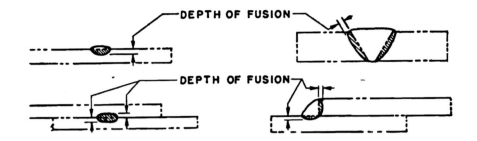

Depth of Fusion

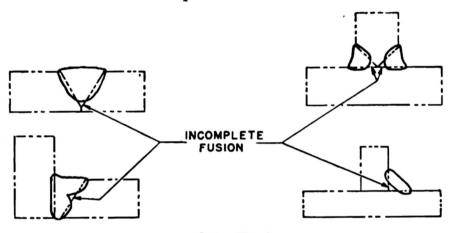

Incomplete Fusion

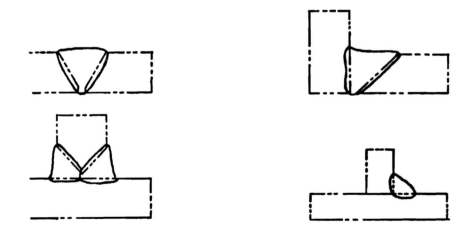

Complete Fusion

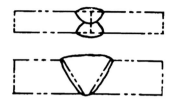

Complete Joint Penetration

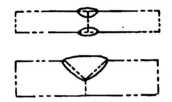

Partial Joint Penetration

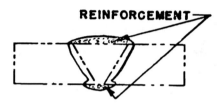

Reinforcement

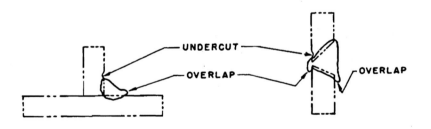

Undercut and Overlap

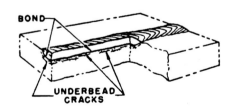

Underbead Cracks

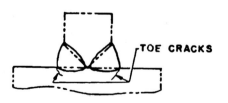

Toe Cracks

183

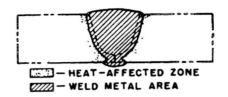

- HEAT-AFFECTED ZONE
- WELD METAL AREA

Heat-Affected Zone and Weld Metal Area

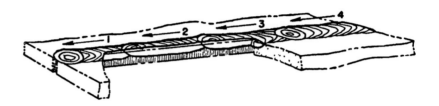

Backstep Sequence

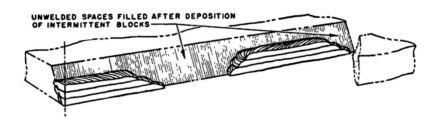

UNWELDED SPACES FILLED AFTER DEPOSITION
OF INTERMITTENT BLOCKS

Block Sequence

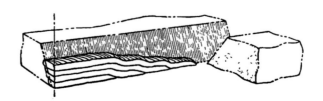

Cascade Sequence

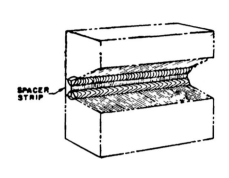

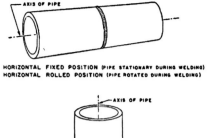

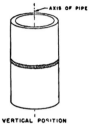

Spacer Strip

Positions of Pipe During
Welding

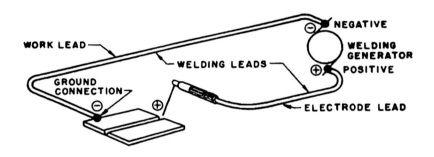

Reverse Polarity

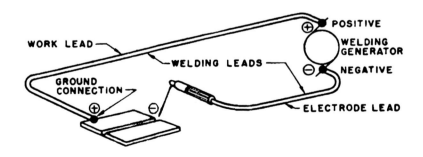

Straight Polarity

STANDARD WELDING SYMBOLS

Basic Welding Symbols and Their Location Significance

Location Significance	Fillet	Plug or Slot	Spot or Projection	Seam	Back or Backing	Surfacing	Scarf for Brazed Joint	Flange Edge
Arrow Side					Groove weld symbol			
Other Side					Groove weld symbol	Not used		Not used
Both Sides	Not used	Not used		Not used		Not used		Not used
No Arrow Side or Other Side Significance	Not used	Not used		Not used		Not used		Not used

Basic Welding Symbols and Their Location Significance

Location Significance		Groove						Flare-V	Flare-Bevel
	Flange Corner	Square	V	Bevel	U	J			
Arrow Side									
Other Side									
Both Sides	Not used								
No Arrow Side or Other Side Significance	Not used							Not used	Not used

Location Significance
- Arrow Side
- Other Side
- Both Sides
- No Arrow Side or Other Side Significance

Supplementary Symbols Used with Welding Symbols

Weld-All-Around Symbol — Weld-all around symbol indicates that weld extends completely around the joint

Convex Contour Symbol — Convex contour symbol indicates face of weld to be finished to convex contour

Joint with Backing — With groove weld symbol. Note: Material and dimensions of backing are specified

Flush Contour Symbol — Flush contour symbol (user's standard) indicates method of obtaining specified contour but not degree of finish

Field Weld Symbol — Field weld symbol indicates that welds are to be made at a place other than that of initial construction

Joint with Spacer — With modified groove weld symbol. Double bevel groove. Note: Material and dimensions of spacer as specified

Melt-Thru Symbol — Any applicable weld symbol. Melt thru symbol is not dimensioned (except height)

Multiple Reference Lines — First operation shown on reference line nearest arrow. Second operation or supplementary data. Third operation or test information.

Complete Penetration — Indicates complete penetration regardless of type of weld or joint preparation

Supplementary Symbols

	Weld-All Around	Field Weld	Melt Thru	Backing, Spacer	Flush	Contour Convex	Concave

Typical Welding Symbols

Square Groove Welding Symbol — Orientation location and all dimensions other than depth of filling are shown on the drawing. Omission of size indicates joint penetration. Root opening

Chain Intermittent Fillet Welding Symbol — Pitch (distance between centers) of increments. Length of increments. Size (length of leg).

Back or Backing Welding Symbol

Staggered Intermittent Fillet Welding Symbol — Size (length of leg). Pitch (distance between centers) of increments. Length of increments.

Plug Welding Symbol — Depth of filling in inches (omission indicates filling is complete). Pitch (distance between centers) of welds. Included angle of countersink. Size (diameter of hole at root).

Backgouging Welding Symbol — Second reference line used for back gouging and welding as a second operation. Process reference must be used to indicate process desired.

Flash or Upset Welding Symbol — No arrow side or other side significance. Process reference must be used to indicate process.

Spot Welding Symbol — Size (diameter of weld). Strength (in lb per weld) may be used instead. Number of welds. Pitch (distance between centers) of weld. Process reference must be used to indicate process.

Seam Welding Symbol — Size (width of weld). Strength (in lb per linear inch) may be used instead. Length of welds or increments. Pitch (distance between centers) of increments. Process reference must be used to indicate process.

Flare V and Flare Bevel Groove Welding Symbols — Root opening. Size is considered as extending only to tangent points.

Edge and Corner Flange Welding Symbols — Radius. Size of weld. Height above point of tangency.

Surfacing Welding Symbol Indicating Built up Surface — Size (height of deposit). Omission indicates no specific height desired.

Single V Groove Welding Symbol Indicating Root Penetration — Root opening. Groove angle. Size. Depth of preparation. Effective throat.

Double Bevel Groove Welding Symbol — Arrow points toward member to be prepared. Omission of size dimension indicates a total depth of preparation equal to thickness of members.

Projection Welding Symbol — Projection welding reference must be used. Diameter of weld may be used instead for circular projection welds.

Double Fillet Welding Symbol — Size (length of leg). Specification process or other reference.

Welding Symbols for Combined Welds — Length of welds or increments. Omission indicates that weld extends between abrupt changes in direction or as dimensioned.

Process Abbreviations
Where process abbreviations are to be included in the tail of the welding symbol reference is made to Table A Designation of Welding and Allied Processes by Letters of AWS 2.4 79 71

AMERICAN WELDING SOCIETY INC
2501 N.W. 7th Street Miami Florida 33125

Location of Elements of a Welding Symbol

- Finish symbol
- Contour symbol
- Root opening, depth of filling for plug and slot welds
- Groove angle, included angle of countersink for plug welds
- Length of weld
- Pitch (center to center spacing) of welds
- Field weld symbol
- Weld all around symbol
- Reference line
- Specification process or other reference
- Tail (Tail omitted when reference is not used)
- Basic weld symbol or detail reference
- Arrow connecting reference line to arrow side member of joint
- Depth of preparation size or strength for certain welds
- Number of spot or projection welds
- Elements in this area remain as shown when tail and arrow are reversed
- (BOTH SIDES) (N) (E) S (F) L–P R (A) (OTHER SIDE) (ARROW SIDE)

Basic Joints—Identification of Arrow Side and Other Side of Joint

Butt Joint — Arrow of welding symbol. Arrow side of joint. Other side of joint.

Corner Joint — Arrow of welding symbol. Arrow side of joint. Other side of joint.

T-Joint — Arrow of welding symbol. Arrow side of joint. Other side of joint.

Lap Joint — Arrow of welding symbol. Arrow side member of joint. Other side member of joint.

Edge Joint — Arrow side of joint. Arrow of welding symbol. Other side member of joint. Joint.

AIDS FOR ARC WELDING PROGRESS

In the interest of scientific and social advancement, the publishers of this book also have for sale other books and bulletins on the various phases of arc welding. The following books, published as a non-profit service, are recommended for engineers, designers, production supervisors, shop men, weldors, students and others seeking advancement through knowledge of arc welding. Please make checks or money orders payable to The Lincoln Electric Company, Cleveland, Ohio 44117. Books are shipped postage paid, book rate, fourth class.

PROCEDURE HANDBOOK OF ARC WELDING

This handbook has become a world-wide reference standard for welding design; now revised for the twelfth time since its original printing in 1933; a 700-page book on all phases of arc welding. Widely used by engineers, designers, production personnel and weldors; over 450,000 copies of the book in print.

Divided by topic into eight parts, each separately indexed and arranged to facilitate study or reference on a subject of particular interest. The alphabetical index for the entire book and separate indexes for each section make it easy to find needed information quickly.

Size — 8½″ × 11″ — Ideal for use in office, shop or school. Bound in semiflexible simulated leather, gold embossed.

Condensed Table of Contents

General — Arc Welding History, Processes, Equipment, Nomenclature.

Production Welding Data — Techniques, Procedures and Costs for Welding Steel (Production information for quality, low-cost welds).

Weldability of Metals — Analysis, Properties, Welding characteristics of all common metals are presented with suggested welding procedures.

Machinery & Structural Design — Complete theoretical and practical design data for efficient use of welded steel.

Weld Quality — Includes review of codes, testing and inspecting.

Application — Typical examples of arc welding applications.

Reference Data

NEW LESSONS IN ARC WELDING

A book of 79 welding lessons plus practical welding information; covers welding mild steel, alloys, sheet metal and pipe; gives new procedures for faster welding, metals identification, joint selection and machine design. 320 pages completely illustrated, over 450 illustrations and drawings. 6″ x 9″ size, bound in simulated gold embossed leather.

THE STABILIZER

"The Stabilizer" published quarterly by Lincoln, is considered by many the official magazine for a vast army of men who weld. Each issue is packed full of practical welding ideas contributed by weldors themselves, promoting good welding and the advancement of the industry. Write for free sample copy. Send name, position and home address to The Lincoln Electric Company, Cleveland, Ohio 44117.

PREHEAT CALCULATOR

A slide rule type of calculator for determining the proper preheat and interpass temperature when welding high carbon and alloy steels that need to be preheated for the best quality welds. Temperature can be calculated for any steel for which the analysis and thickness is known; eliminates guessing.

INCENTIVE MANAGEMENT

Mr. Lincoln explains his philosophy of how workers and managers in business and industry can develop their skills and work together cooperatively to everyone's benefit, rather than at cross purposes to everyone's expense. Tells how, with incentives and business, we can have high wages without high prices; how incentives can be put into any business, large or small. 6″ × 9″ page size, 288 pages; bound in gold embossed cloth covered board.

A NEW APPROACH TO INDUSTRIAL ECONOMICS

A book for everyone who works for a living, by James F. Lincoln, past-Chairman, The Lincoln Electric Company. The ideas of James F. Lincoln, expressed in this book with the authority of his 53 years of executive leadership, require and deserve careful reading. The problems to which he addresses himself are much discussed, generate strong convictions, and are among the most vital facing our country today. His straight-forward, logical and time-tested answers are important to every citizen of the United States. Order your copy today!

THE JAMES F. LINCOLN ARC WELDING FOUNDATION

The James F. Lincoln Arc Welding Foundation was created in 1936 through a deed of trust, "to encourage and stimulate scientific interest in and scientific study, research and education in respect of the development of the arc welding industry through advance in the knowledge and design and practical application of the arc welding process." As a contribution to science and to promote industrial progress through education, the Foundation produces and publishes the books listed here as a non-profit service to the industry. Please make checks or money orders payable to The James F. Lincoln Arc Welding Foundation, Cleveland, Ohio 44117.

METALS AND HOW TO WELD THEM, SECOND EDITION

Published as a combination text and reference book to give all uses of welding, practical information for making better welds at lower costs. It explains in clear, logical, easily understood steps the structure and properties of metals, what happens to the internal structure during welding and how to weld metals correctly.

The first six chapters discuss metals, their mechanical interests, properties and how they are used. Also discussed are the fundamentals of metallurgy and their significance for welding. This information is then related to correct welding procedures for steels of low, medium and high carbon, stainless, manganese, high chromium and tool and die steel, cast iron and hardsurfacing. Final section includes suggestions for making good welds, glossary of welding terms, and useful data. 400 pages with 190 drawings, photographs and tables.

HOW THE BLUEPRINT IS MADE

Perhaps it would be well to tell how a blueprint is made and thus satisfy a natural curiosity in the reader's mind.

Blueprints are made in much the same manner that a photograph print is made. First a drawing of the object is made by the draftsman. Second, a tracing of this drawing is made with ink on a fine thread fabric which is made translucent and paper-like with a starch preparation and is named, descriptively, tracing cloth. This may be likened to the photograph negative. Third, the blueprint is made like a contact print from a photograph negative. The tracing being placed upon sensitized paper (chemically treated to change color when exposed to light) and the combination exposed to light rays.

When this paper is washed, the unexposed surfaces, which have been directly beneath the lines and inked parts of the tracing, remain white. The exposed surfaces become blue and the drawing appears as white lines on a blue background. Innumerable prints may be made from the same tracing.

There are other methods of printing drawings which see extensive use today.

Van Dyke paper - used to obtain reversed tracings (light lines on a dark background) and making it possible to make blueprints with blue lines on a white background. No actual tracing is necessary.

Photostat prints - made directly from the drawing to any desired size- a photographic process resulting in white lines on a dark background.

B. W. paper produces black lines on white background directly from the drawing.

Also various methods of copying such as ditto and mimeograph.

These direct printing papers are gaining much popularity as their use eliminates the tracing, which was a bothersome and expensive item to produce in the older process.

187

DESIGN OF WELDMENTS

Theoretical analysis and case history studies explain how to design machine components for manufacturing economies and improvement of product performance through efficient use of steel's excellent physical properties. Text covers designing for fatigue, tension, compression, deflection, impact, vibration and torsional load condition. 464 pages, 923 illustrations, 24 full-size nomographs, 8½" × 11" page size; bound in gold embossed cloth covered board.

DESIGN OF WELDED STRUCTURES

Presents methods of designing with arc welded steel for buildings, bridges, towers, containers and all types of miscellaneous structures. The methods described can be applied to the whole structure or its component parts. Load and stress analysis, column related design, girder related design, welded connection design, joint design and production, reference design formulas are thoroughly presented. This 8½" × 11" 832 page book contains 966 drawings, 28 nomographs, 163 tables, 190 charts and 145 photographs. Seven "working sections" contain detailed and practical examples showing how to create more efficient designs that can be fabricated more economically.

ARC WELDING INSTRUCTION FOR THE BEGINNER

Basic skill instruction for industrial, vocational, apprentice and in-plant training programs — 80 to 100 hours class time contained in a series of 21 lessons on the basic arc welding skills. The mastery of each lesson is one step toward learning how to arc weld in all positions. The book takes the beginner by the shortest possible route from the study of certain process fundamentals to learning to strike an arc and run a bead to the advanced techniques of vertical and overhead welding. Discussions concentrate on describing the manipulative skills for the basic weld types — fillet, lap, and butt welds, in the various positions — flat, vertical, overhead and horizontal. Technical discussions on process applications, type of electrodes, machines and basic metallurgy are intentionally brief. The author believes this related information, though important, can be more quickly covered and better understood if it is presented after a student learns to weld. Teacher's Manual also available.

ARC WELDING LESSONS FOR SCHOOL & FARM SHOP

Eight informational lessons and six skill lessons introduce both high school and college students to basic techniques for arc welding in all positions. Later lessons deal with special skills like hardsurfacing, welding cast iron and others. Each chapter is complete in itself, but if studied in sequence, the chapters make a complete course. Each chapter features a teaching guide with outlines for the lesson; points out clearly the objective of that particular lesson; list key points, materials needed and suggestions for jobs. There are 343 pages of lesson material, each 6" × 9" in size, with illustrations, photographs, exercises and projects.

CPSIA information can be obtained at www.ICGtesting.com
Printed in the USA
BVOW04s2335180516

448560BV00007B/125/P